Pillsbury

fast slow cooker
cookbook

15-minute prep and
your slow cooker does the rest!

WILEY

Wiley Publishing, Inc.

For general information on our other products and services or for technical support, please contact our Customer Care Department within the United States at (800) 762-2974, outside the United States at (317) 572-3993 or fax (317) 572-4002.

Wiley also publishes its books in a variety of electronic formats. Some content that appears in print may not be available in electronic books. For more information about Wiley products, visit our web site at www.wiley.com.

Library of Congress Cataloging-in-Publication Data:

Pillsbury fast slow cooker cookbook / Pillsbury editors.

p. cm.

Includes index.

ISBN 978-0-471-75310-0 (paper)

1. Electric cookery, Slow. I. Pillsbury Company.

TX827.P554 2009

641.5'884—dc22

2008007356

Printed in China

10 9 8 7 6 5 4 3 2 1

Cover photo: Biscuit Chicken Pot Pie, page 22

General Mills:

Pillsbury Kitchens:

Editorial Director: Jeff Nowak

Manager and Editor, Cookbooks: Lois Tlusty

Food Editor: Lola Whalen

Recipe Development and Testing: Pillsbury Kitchens

Photography:

Photography: General Mills Photography Studios and Image Library

Photographer: Val Bourassa

Food Stylists: Nancy Johnson, Sue Finley

Wiley Publishing, Inc.:

Publisher: Natalie Chapman

Executive Editor: Anne Ficklen

Editor: Adam Kowit

Production Editor: Alda Trabucchi

Cover Design: Suzanne Sunwoo

Art Director: Tai Blanche

Interior Design and Layout: Holly Wittenberg and Erin Zeltner

Photography Art Direction: Lynn Dolan

Manufacturing Manager: Kevin Watt

Home of the Pillsbury Bake-Off® Contest

Our recipes have been tested in the Pillsbury Kitchens and meet our standards of easy preparation, reliability and great taste.

For more great recipes, visit pillsbury.com

Welcome...
From the Pillsbury Kitchens
Home of the Pillsbury Bake-Off® Contest

Fast slow cooking—seems like an oxymoron?

With *Pillsbury Fast Slow Cooker Cookbook*, you can have the best of both worlds. Every recipe is fast to prep (15 minutes or less) and cooks slowly in your slow cooker.

Hitting that snooze button may be more tempting in the morning than heading to the kitchen. But come on, rise and shine! It will be worth the extra 15 minutes to be greeted with the aroma of dinner cooking at the end of a busy day.

Peek inside, and you'll find a recipe for a family night dinner or a quiet evening meal with friends. Need a side dish to go with grilled chicken? Take your pick. Check out each Quick Tip for recipe serving ideas, ingredient substitutions and success hints.

Fast slow cooking is the only way to go!

Warmly,
The Pillsbury Editors

table of contents

secrets for slow cooking success

Slow Cooker Tips

A slow cooker is the answer for getting home-cooked meals on the table even on the busiest days. Use these sure-fire tips for preparing recipes successfully in your slow cooker.

Size of the slow cooker is important so be sure to use the size that is called for in the recipe.

Filling the slow cooker two-thirds to three-fourths full is ideal, but being half full will also work.

Cleanup is easier if you coat the inside of the slow cooker with cooking spray before adding the food.

Root vegetables, such as carrots and potatoes, should be cut into small pieces of equal size and placed on the bottom of the slow cooker. Add meat, seasonings and other vegetables and liquid on top of the root vegetables.

Tender vegetables, such as fresh mushrooms and zucchini, which require shorter cooking time, should be added at the end to retain color, texture and flavor.

Prevent potatoes from darkening by covering them with a liquid in the slow cooker.

Frozen foods, such as vegetables, should be thawed before adding them to the slow cooker unless they are added near the end of the cook time.

Browning meats before placing them in a slow cooker is often recommended for better color, which can improve the flavor and appearance of the finished dish. However, it isn't necessary to brown meat before slow cooking, except for ground meats.

Trim excess fat from meats and poultry to reduce fat in the finished dish. If there is too much fat, skim it from the surface using a spoon or a slice of bread.

Use dried leaf herbs instead of ground because they add more flavor during the long cooking time.

Red pepper becomes stronger and bitter during long cooking times so use smaller amounts of ground red pepper (cayenne) and red pepper sauce. Taste the food before serving to determine whether more seasoning is needed.

Save time in the morning by cutting up vegetables, such as carrots and onions, and refrigerate them overnight in a covered container or sealed food-storage plastic bag.

Cooked food can be held up to an hour on the Low setting without overcooking.

Liquids don't evaporate during slow cooking so do not add extra liquid even if the ingredients may appear dry before cooking. It is best to follow the recipe.

Lifting the lid releases the heat and increases cooking time by about 20 minutes. If your slow cooker is round, try spinning the glass lid during cooking to have moisture fall off so you can see inside.

Cook times in ranges, such as 8 to 10 hours, will have different results. After 8 hours of cooking, large pieces of meat can still usually be sliced, but after 10 hours, the meat will shred. Both will be tasty but the appearance will be different.

Food Safety Counts

Play it safe and check this list of food safety guidelines before you use your slow cooker.

- Don't cook frozen meat in the slow cooker because it takes too long to reach a safe temperature. Thaw meat and poultry in the refrigerator or in a microwave oven following the manufacturer's directions.

- Cook and drain all ground meats before adding them to the slow cooker to destroy any bacteria that the meat may contain. **Immediately** place the cooked ground meat in the slow cooker to finish cooking. **Never** cook and refrigerate ground meat to finish cooking later.

- Don't cook whole poultry, such as chicken, turkey and Rock Cornish hens, in the slow cooker because it takes too long for a safe cooking temperature to reach the bone.

- It is important that the lid fit securely on the slow cooker. The lid holds in the heat, allowing for safe cooking temperatures to be reached and maintained.

- The temperature in the center of the food being cooked should reach 130 to 140°F within three to four hours or approximately halfway through the cooking period. At the end of the cooking time, the food must be at least 160 to 165°F in the center, 170°F for poultry breast, 180°F for dark meat poultry.

- Don't use frozen ingredients.

- Don't assemble the ingredients and refrigerate ahead of time. You can prep some of the ingredients (peel and cut up vegetables) and refrigerate ahead. Just don't combine them until you are ready to turn on the slow cooker.

- Perishable ingredients such as meat and poultry can be used right from the refrigerator.

- Only remove the lid to check for doneness at the minimum cook time. It is estimated that the temperature drops about 10°F every time the lid is removed and it takes about 20 minutes to recover the temperature.

Make It To Go

A slow cooker is the perfect appliance to take to potlucks, family gatherings or office events.

- Wrap the slow cooker in a towel or newspaper to keep it warm. Place it in a box or other container that will stay flat in your car.

- Attach rubber bands around the handles and lid to secure the lid when traveling and prevent spills.

- Serve the cooked food within an hour, or plug in the slow cooker and set on the Low (or keep warm) setting to keep the food warm for hours.

- It is important not to undercook foods. For food-safety reasons, slow cooker recipes containing raw poultry or meat should cook a minimum of three hours.

- Don't use your slow cooker as a storage container. Remove leftovers from the slow cooker and refrigerate or freeze as soon as you are finished eating. Cooked food shouldn't stand at room temperature longer than one hour.

- Food should not be reheated in the slow cooker. Instead, reheat food on top of the stove or in the microwave.

Dress It Up

Flavors meld together during slow cooking but the colors of some ingredients fade. Dress up the dish before serving with a sprinkle of:

- Chopped green onions, parsley, chives or other fresh herbs
- Chopped red, yellow or green bell peppers
- Cherry tomato halves or chopped tomatoes
- Shredded cheese
- Chopped olives
- A dollop of sour cream or plain yogurt
- Paprika or chili powder
- Crushed tortilla or corn chips
- Chopped or slivered toasted nuts

- Determine if your slow cooker temperature is accurate by filling it with two quarts of water and heating on the Low setting for eight hours. Quickly measure the water temperature with an accurate instant read thermometer. The temperature of the water should be 180°F, taking into consideration the minor heat loss from removing the lid.

How to Adapt Your Recipes for a Slow Cooker

When you want to change your favorite recipe to a slow cooker recipe, here are a few things to consider.

1. Look for a similar recipe in this cookbook to use as a guide for quantities, amount of liquid and cooking time.

2. Unless you are adapting a soup recipe, reduce the amount of liquid by about half because liquids do not boil away as in other methods of cooking.

3. If you are adapting a soup recipe, use the same amount of liquid as called for in the recipe.

4. Use less-expensive cuts of meat, such as beef round steak, beef chuck roast or pork boneless shoulder roast, which will work well in the moist heat and low temperatures of the slow cooker.

5. Trim as much visible fat from meat and poultry before cooking so there is less fat to remove from the finished dish.

6. Instead of using fresh dairy products, such as milk or sour cream, which can curdle, try canned condensed soups, nonfat milk powder or canned evaporated milk.

7. For best results, add cheese, sour cream or cream during the last 30 minutes of cooking time or just before serving to prevent them from breaking down.

8. If poultry is browned before placing in the slow cooker, remove the skin before browning. This not only helps to reduce excess fat but it also improves the appearance.

9. Dense root vegetables, such as carrots, potatoes and turnips, often take longer than meat to cook in a slow cooker. Cut the vegetables into smaller, bite-sized pieces and place them in the bottom of the slow cooker. The juices from the meat will drip down and help the vegetables cook.

10. The flavor of dried basil seems to strengthen during long cooking. If adapting a recipe using dried basil, you may want to cut the amount in half.

11. Ground red pepper (cayenne) and red pepper sauce tend to strengthen and become bitter during long slow cooking. You may want to cut the amount in half and then taste the dish before serving to determine if more flavor is needed.

Slow Cooking at High Altitude

Living at higher altitudes (3,500 feet and above) can present unique slow cooking challenges. Because recipes vary, there are no set rules that fit all recipes, so sometimes trial and error is the best teaching tool. Here are some guidelines that should help:

The Power Goes Off

If you aren't at home, it is best not to eat the food cooking in the slow cooker. It may look done but the food may have stood at too low a temperature to be safe.

If you are home, remove the food from the slow cooker and cook it in another pan on a gas stove or outdoor grill. Or store it in a cooler with ice if you have no way to cook it.

If you know the food is completely cooked, it can safely stay in the cooker up to two hours with the power off. Don't lift the lid so the temperature drops.

- Most foods take longer to cook, particularly meats cooked in boiling liquid. The time may be up to twice as long as the recipe suggests for meats to become tender. Try cooking meats on the High setting instead of on Low to shorten the cooking time.

- Dried beans will also cook more slowly. Try using the overnight soaking in water method before cooking them in the slow cooker.

- Cutting vegetables into smaller pieces than the recipe suggests will help them cook more quickly.

- Call your local U.S. Department of Agriculture (USDA) Extension Services, listed in the phone book under "County Government," with questions about using your slow cooker at high altitude.

chapter one

family favorite chicken & turkey

prep time
15 minutes

start to finish
4 hours 30 minutes

slow cooker
5 to 6 quart

6 servings

Herbed Chicken and Stuffing Supper

3 lb bone-in chicken pieces, skin removed

1 can (10¾ oz) condensed cream of chicken with herbs soup

4 medium dark-orange sweet potatoes, peeled, cut into ½-inch slices

1 package (6 oz) chicken-flavor stuffing mix

1¼ cups water

¼ cup butter or margarine, melted

1 cup frozen cut green beans, thawed

1. In 5- to 6-quart slow cooker, place chicken pieces. Spoon soup over chicken. Top with sweet potatoes. In medium bowl, mix stuffing mix, water and melted butter. Spoon over sweet potatoes.

2. Cover; cook on Low heat setting 4 to 6 hours.

3. About 20 minutes before serving, sprinkle green beans over stuffing. Cover; cook on Low heat setting 15 to 20 minutes longer or until beans are tender.

1 Serving: Calories 500; Total Fat 19g (Saturated Fat 8g; Trans Fat 0.5g); Cholesterol 100mg; Sodium 990mg; Total Carbohydrate 51g (Dietary Fiber 5g) **Exchanges:** 3 Starch, ½ Other Carbohydrate, 3 Lean Meat, 1½ Fat **Carbohydrate Choices:** 3½

QuickTip

Adding the green beans at the end of the cook time keeps them green and tender. You can add the beans with the sweet potatoes, but they will be softer in texture and have a lighter green color.

prep time
15 minutes

start to finish
7 hours 15 minutes

slow cooker
5 to 6 quart

6 servings

Chicken with Twenty Cloves of Garlic

1 teaspoon salt

1 teaspoon paprika

½ teaspoon pepper

1 teaspoon olive oil

1 cut-up whole chicken (3 to 3½ lb)

1 large onion, sliced

1 medium bulb garlic (about 20 cloves)

1. In small bowl, mix salt, paprika, pepper and oil to form paste; spread evenly over each piece of chicken.

2. In 5- to 6-quart slow cooker, place onion slices. Arrange chicken over onion. Separate garlic into cloves; do not peel cloves. Place cloves around chicken. Cover; cook on Low heat setting 7 to 8 hours.

3. With slotted spoon, remove chicken, onion and garlic from slow cooker; place on serving platter. Squeeze garlic cloves to use on chicken.

1 Serving: Calories 170; Total Fat 7g (Saturated Fat 1.5g; Trans Fat 0g); Cholesterol 70mg; Sodium 460mg; Total Carbohydrate 4g (Dietary Fiber 0g) **Exchanges:** 3 Lean Meat **Carbohydrate Choices:** 0

QuickTip

A whole bulb of garlic seems like a lot of garlic, but the flavor dissipates during the long cooking. The cooked garlic is also good squeezed on mashed potatoes or slices of crusty bread.

Cajun-Seasoned Chicken

3 slices bacon, cut up

½ cup chopped green bell pepper

¼ cup chopped onion

¼ cup chopped celery

1¼ lb boneless skinless chicken thighs

2 teaspoons Cajun seasoning

1 can (14.5 oz) diced tomatoes, undrained

1⅓ cups uncooked regular long-grain white rice

2⅔ cups water

1. In 10-inch nonstick skillet, cook bacon over medium-high heat until crisp. Add bell pepper, onion and celery; cook 2 to 3 minutes longer or until crisp-tender. With slotted spoon, spoon bacon and vegetables into 3½- or 4-quart slow cooker.

2. Sprinkle chicken thighs with 1 teaspoon of the Cajun seasoning; place in same skillet. Cook chicken 4 to 5 minutes, turning once, until browned on both sides. Arrange chicken and any remaining drippings over vegetables in slow cooker. Pour tomatoes over chicken. Stir in remaining teaspoon Cajun seasoning.

3. Cover; cook on Low heat setting 8 to 9 hours.

4. About 30 minutes before serving time, cook rice in water as directed on package. Serve chicken and sauce over rice.

1 Serving: Calories 520; Total Fat 15g (Saturated Fat 4.5g; Trans Fat 0g); Cholesterol 95mg; Sodium 630mg; Total Carbohydrate 59g (Dietary Fiber 2g) **Exchanges:** 3 Starch, ½ Other Carbohydrate, 1 Vegetable, 4 Lean Meat **Carbohydrate Choices:** 4

QuickTip

To add a little more heat to this Cajun dish, shake in a few drops of red pepper sauce before serving.

Chicken and Noodles Alfredo

1 lb boneless skinless chicken thighs, cut into ¾-inch pieces

1 can (14 oz) quartered artichokes, drained

1 jar (16 oz) Alfredo pasta sauce

1 cup water

½ cup chopped sun-dried tomatoes (not in oil)

3 cups uncooked medium egg noodles (5 oz)

2 tablespoons shredded Parmesan cheese

1. In 3- to 4-quart slow cooker, mix chicken, artichokes, pasta sauce and water.

2. Cover; cook on Low heat setting 5 to 6 hours.

3. About 25 minutes before serving, stir tomatoes and uncooked noodles into chicken mixture.

4. Increase heat setting to High. Cover; cook 15 to 20 minutes longer or until noodles are tender. Sprinkle cheese over individual servings.

1 Serving: Calories 480; Total Fat 26g (Saturated Fat 11g; Trans Fat 0g); Cholesterol 155mg; Sodium 950mg; Total Carbohydrate 33g (Dietary Fiber 4g) **Exchanges:** 1½ Starch, ½ Other Carbohydrate, 3½ Lean Meat, 3 Fat **Carbohydrate Choices:** 2

QuickTip

Pasta quickly absorbs the sauce in this dish if it has to stand before serving. For a creamy consistency, stir in a little hot water.

Chicken Italiano

8 boneless skinless chicken thighs (1½ to 1¾ lb)

½ cup chopped onion

½ cup halved pitted ripe olives

2 tablespoons capers

1 teaspoon dried oregano leaves

½ teaspoon salt

½ teaspoon dried rosemary leaves, crushed

¼ teaspoon garlic powder

1 can (14.5 oz) diced tomatoes, undrained

¼ cup water

1 tablespoon cornstarch

1. In 3½- to 4-quart slow cooker, place chicken thighs. Top with onion, olives and capers. Sprinkle with oregano, salt, rosemary and garlic powder. Pour tomatoes over chicken.

2. Cover; cook on Low heat setting 7 to 10 hours.

3. About 15 minutes before serving, with slotted spoon, remove chicken and vegetables from slow cooker; place on serving platter. Cover to keep warm.

4. In small bowl, blend water and cornstarch until smooth. Stir into liquid in slow cooker. Increase heat setting to High. Cover; cook 5 to 10 minutes longer or until thickened. Serve chicken with sauce.

1 Serving: Calories 330; Total Fat 16g (Saturated Fat 4.5g; Trans Fat 0g); Cholesterol 105mg; Sodium 780mg; Total Carbohydrate 10g (Dietary Fiber 2g) **Exchanges:** ½ Other Carbohydrate, 5½ Lean Meat **Carbohydrate Choices:** ½

Chicken and Roasted Vegetables Dinner

1 lb unpeeled small potatoes (6 to 8), cut into 1-inch pieces (3 cups)

2 cups ready-to-eat baby-cut carrots

1 cup frozen small whole onions (from 1-lb bag), thawed

6 boneless skinless chicken thighs (1¼ lb)

½ teaspoon salt

⅛ teaspoon pepper

1 jar (12 oz) chicken gravy

1½ cups frozen sweet peas, thawed

1. Spray 3- to 4-quart slow cooker with cooking spray. Place potatoes, carrots and onions in slow cooker. Sprinkle chicken thighs with salt and pepper; place over vegetables in slow cooker. Pour gravy over top.

2. Cover; cook on Low heat setting 8 to 10 hours.

3. Stir in peas. Increase heat setting to High. Cover; cook about 15 minutes longer or until peas are tender.

1 Serving: Calories 310; Total Fat 11g (Saturated Fat 3g; Trans Fat 0g); Cholesterol 60mg; Sodium 630mg; Total Carbohydrate 28g (Dietary Fiber 4g) **Exchanges:** 1 Starch, ½ Other Carbohydrate, 1½ Vegetable, 2½ Lean Meat, ½ Fat **Carbohydrate Choices:** 2

QuickTip

Place the peas in the refrigerator to thaw when you start the slow cooker in the morning. They'll be ready to add at the end of the cook time.

prep time
10 minutes

start to finish
7 hours 20 minutes

slow cooker
3½ to 6 quart

5 servings

Chicken with Creamy Paprika Sauce

10 bone-in chicken thighs (about 2½ lb), skin removed

1 medium onion, sliced

3 tablespoons chicken broth or water

2 tablespoons paprika

½ teaspoon salt

3 tablespoons cold water

3 tablespoons cornstarch

1 container (8 oz) sour cream with chives

1. In 3½- to 6-quart slow cooker, place chicken thighs and onion. In small bowl, mix broth and paprika. Pour over chicken. Sprinkle with salt.

2. Cover; cook on Low heat setting 7 to 8 hours.

3. About 15 minutes before serving, with slotted spoon, remove chicken and onion from slow cooker; place on serving platter. Cover to keep warm.

4. In small bowl, blend water and cornstarch until smooth. Stir into liquid in slow cooker. Increase heat setting to High. Cover; cook 8 to 10 minutes longer or until thickened. Stir in sour cream. Pour sauce over chicken.

1 Serving: Calories 340; Total Fat 20g (Saturated Fat 9g; Trans Fat 0.5g); Cholesterol 115mg; Sodium 370mg; Total Carbohydrate 10g (Dietary Fiber 1g) **Exchanges:** ½ Starch, 4 Lean Meat, 1½ Fat **Carbohydrate Choices:** ½

QuickTip

If you can't find sour cream with chives, sometimes labeled as "potato topping," use an eight-ounce container of sour cream and add one tablespoon chopped fresh or dried chives. To save time in the morning, remove the skin from the chicken the night before.

Thai Peanut Chicken

8 bone-in chicken thighs (about 2 lb), skin removed

¾ cup hot chunky-style salsa

¼ cup peanut butter

2 tablespoons lime juice

1 tablespoon soy sauce

1 teaspoon grated gingerroot

¼ cup chopped peanuts

2 tablespoons chopped fresh cilantro

1. In 3½- to 6-quart slow cooker, place chicken thighs. In small bowl, mix salsa, peanut butter, lime juice, soy sauce and gingerroot. Pour over chicken.

2. Cover; cook on Low heat setting 8 to 9 hours.

3. With slotted spoon, remove chicken from slow cooker; place on serving platter. Skim fat from sauce. Spoon sauce over chicken. Sprinkle with peanuts and cilantro.

1 Serving: Calories 410; Total Fat 25g (Saturated Fat 6g; Trans Fat 0g); Cholesterol 90mg; Sodium 700mg; Total Carbohydrate 8g (Dietary Fiber 2g) Exchanges: ½ Other Carbohydrate, 5½ Lean Meat, 1½ Fat Carbohydrate Choices: ½

QuickTip

Serve with Jasmine rice and a simple side of sliced cucumbers tossed with vinaigrette for a truly Thai meal.

Biscuit Chicken Pot Pie

1¼ lb boneless skinless chicken thighs

½ cup chopped onion

½ teaspoon poultry seasoning

½ teaspoon dried thyme leaves

¼ teaspoon pepper

1 jar (18 oz) chicken gravy

2 medium stalks celery, cut into ½-inch slices (1 cup)

1 bag (1 lb) frozen mixed vegetables

6 large frozen flaky biscuits (from 22.1-oz bag)

1. Spray 3½- to 4-quart slow cooker with cooking spray. Place chicken in cooker. Top with onion, poultry seasoning, thyme, pepper, gravy and celery.

2. Cover; cook on Low heat setting 8 to 10 hours.

3. Gently stir frozen vegetables into chicken mixture. Increase heat setting to High. Cover; cook 30 minutes longer.

4. Meanwhile, heat oven to 375°F. Bake biscuits as directed on bag.

5. Split biscuits. Spoon about 1 cup chicken mixture on bottom half of each biscuit; top with remaining halves.

1 Serving: Calories 450; Total Fat 22g (Saturated Fat 7g; Trans Fat 2.5g); Cholesterol 60mg; Sodium 1080mg; Total Carbohydrate 37g (Dietary Fiber 4g) **Exchanges:** 1½ Starch, ½ Other Carbohydrate, 1 Vegetable, 3 Lean Meat, 2½ Fat **Carbohydrate Choices:** 2½

Chicken Drumsticks with Sweet Potatoes and Pineapple

2 medium dark-orange sweet potatoes, peeled, sliced (about 3 cups)

1 can (8 oz) pineapple tidbits in unsweetened juice, undrained

½ cup chicken broth

¼ cup finely chopped onion

1 teaspoon grated gingerroot, if desired

¼ cup barbecue sauce

2 tablespoons honey

½ teaspoon ground mustard

8 chicken drumsticks (about 1½ lb), skin removed

1. In 3½- to 4-quart slow cooker, mix sweet potatoes, pineapple with juice, broth, onion and gingerroot.

2. In small bowl, mix barbecue sauce, honey and ground mustard. Coat chicken drumsticks well with barbecue sauce mixture. Arrange chicken in single layer over potato mixture in slow cooker, overlapping slightly if necessary. Spoon any remaining barbecue sauce mixture over chicken.

3. Cover; cook on Low heat setting 7 to 10 hours.

1 Serving: Calories 380; Total Fat 6g (Saturated Fat 2g; Trans Fat 0g); Cholesterol 140mg; Sodium 420mg; Total Carbohydrate 43g (Dietary Fiber 3g) Exchanges: 2 Starch, 1 Other Carbohydrate, 4½ Very Lean Meat Carbohydrate Choices: 3

QuickTip

There are two types of sweet potatoes available in most supermarkets. Dark-skinned sweet potatoes with deep orange flesh are moister and sweeter than the pale-skinned variety with light yellow flesh. For this recipe, the dark-skinned sweet potatoes are ideal.

Chicken Legs with Herbed Onion Sauce

10 chicken drumsticks (about 2 lb), skin removed

2 cups frozen small whole onions (from 1-lb bag), thawed

¼ cup dry white wine or chicken broth

¼ cup evaporated milk

2 tablespoons chopped fresh parsley or 2 teaspoons dried parsley flakes

1 teaspoon dried tarragon leaves

¼ teaspoon salt

¼ teaspoon dried rosemary leaves, crushed

1 can (10¾ oz) condensed cream of chicken soup

1. In 3½- to 6-quart slow cooker, place chicken drumsticks. In medium bowl, mix remaining ingredients. Pour over chicken.

2. Cover; cook on Low heat setting 4 to 5 hours.

1 Serving: Calories 260; Total Fat 9g (Saturated Fat 3g; Trans Fat 0g); Cholesterol 105mg; Sodium 640mg; Total Carbohydrate 15g (Dietary Fiber 1g) **Exchanges:** ½ Other Carbohydrate, 1 Vegetable, 4 Very Lean Meat, 1½ Fat **Carbohydrate Choices:** 1

QuickTip

Save extra time in the morning by removing the skin and any fat from the drumsticks the night before.

prep time
15 minutes

start to finish
6 hours 15 minutes

slow cooker
3½ to 4 quart

6 servings

Spanish Chicken

1¾ lb boneless skinless chicken breasts, cut into 1-inch pieces

1 lb Italian turkey sausage links, cut into 1-inch pieces

1 large red bell pepper, chopped (1½ cups)

1 cup chopped onions

2 cloves garlic, finely chopped

1 teaspoon dried oregano leaves

½ to 1 teaspoon crushed red pepper flakes

1 can (28 oz) diced tomatoes, undrained

1 can (6 oz) tomato paste

1 cup uncooked regular long-grain white rice

2 cups water

1 can (14 oz) quartered artichoke hearts, drained

1 can (4 oz) sliced ripe olives, drained

1. Spray 3½- to 4-quart slow cooker with cooking spray. Mix chicken, sausage, bell pepper, onions, garlic, oregano, pepper flakes, tomatoes and tomato paste in slow cooker. Cover; cook on Low heat setting 6 to 8 hours.

2. About 25 minutes before serving, cook rice in 2 cups water as directed on package.

3. Just before serving, stir artichoke hearts and olives into chicken mixture. Cover; cook until hot. Serve chicken mixture with rice.

1 Serving: Calories 510; Total Fat 14g (Saturated Fat 3.5g; Trans Fat 0g); Cholesterol 120mg; Sodium 1540mg; Total Carbohydrate 49g (Dietary Fiber 7g) Exchanges: 2 Starch, ½ Other Carbohydrate, 2 Vegetable, 5 Very Lean Meat, 2 Fat Carbohydrate Choices: 3

Italian Turkey Dinner

2 bone-in turkey thighs (about 1½ lb), skin removed

1 can (14.5 oz) diced tomatoes with Italian-style herbs, undrained

2 tablespoons tomato paste

2 cloves garlic, finely chopped

1 cup uncooked couscous

1½ cups water

2 cups sliced zucchini

1. In 3½- to 4-quart slow cooker, place turkey thighs. In small bowl, mix tomatoes, tomato paste and garlic. Pour over turkey.

2. Cover; cook on Low heat setting 6 to 8 hours.

3. About 25 minutes before serving, cook couscous in water as directed on package. Increase heat setting on slow cooker to High. Stir zucchini into tomato mixture. Cover; cook about 20 minutes longer or until zucchini is tender.

4. To serve, remove bones from turkey. Stir gently to break up turkey. Serve over couscous.

1 Serving: Calories 270; Total Fat 4.5g (Saturated Fat 1.5g; Trans Fat 0g); Cholesterol 100mg; Sodium 210mg; Total Carbohydrate 28g (Dietary Fiber 2g) **Exchanges:** 1½ Starch, 1 Vegetable, 3½ Very Lean Meat **Carbohydrate Choices:** 2

One-Pot Turkey Dinner

3 medium dark-orange sweet
    potatoes, peeled, cut into
    2-inch pieces

3 bone-in turkey thighs (about
    2¼ lb), skin removed

1 jar (12 oz) turkey gravy

2 tablespoons all-purpose flour

1 teaspoon dried parsley flakes

½ teaspoon dried rosemary leaves,
    crushed

⅛ teaspoon pepper

1 box (10 oz) frozen cut green beans

1. In 4- to 5-quart slow cooker, place sweet potatoes. Top with turkey thighs. In small bowl, mix remaining ingredients except beans until smooth. Pour over turkey.

2. Cover; cook on High heat setting 1 hour. Reduce heat setting to low; cook 5 hours longer.

3. One to 2 hours before serving, stir beans into turkey mixture. Cover; cook on Low heat setting 1 to 2 hours longer.

4. With slotted spoon, remove turkey and vegetables from slow cooker; place on serving platter. Remove turkey meat from bones and cut into pieces; discard bones. Stir sauce. Serve turkey and vegetables with sauce.

1 Serving: Calories 340; Total Fat 9g (Saturated Fat 3g; Trans Fat 0g); Cholesterol 155mg; Sodium 460mg; Total Carbohydrate 21g (Dietary Fiber 3g) Exchanges: 1 Starch, ½ Other Carbohydrate, 5½ Very Lean Meat, 1 Fat Carbohydrate Choices: 1½

Turkey with Cornmeal-Thyme Dumplings

TURKEY

2 boneless turkey thighs (about 1½ lb), skin removed

1 can (15.25 oz) whole kernel corn, undrained

1 can (8 oz) tomato sauce

2 tablespoons all-purpose flour

1¼ teaspoons salt

1 teaspoon chili powder

¼ teaspoon pepper

1 medium zucchini, sliced (2 cups)

DUMPLINGS

¼ cup finely chopped onion

½ cup all-purpose flour

½ cup yellow cornmeal

1 teaspoon baking powder

¼ teaspoon salt

¼ teaspoon ground thyme

¼ cup milk

2 tablespoons vegetable oil

1 egg

1. In 3½- to 6-quart slow cooker, place turkey. In small bowl, mix corn, tomato sauce, 2 tablespoons flour, 1 teaspoon of salt, chili powder and pepper. Pour over turkey.

2. Cover; cook on Low heat setting 8 to 10 hours.

3. About 50 minutes before serving, in medium bowl, mix dumpling ingredients. Drop dough by spoonfuls onto hot turkey mixture. Arrange zucchini slices around dumplings; sprinkle with remaining ¼ teaspoon salt. Increase heat setting to High. Cover; cook 35 to 45 minutes longer or until toothpick inserted in center of dumplings comes out clean.

1 Serving: Calories 520; Total Fat 15g (Saturated Fat 3.5g; Trans Fat 0g); Cholesterol 190mg; Sodium 1610mg; Total Carbohydrate 53g (Dietary Fiber 5g) **Exchanges:** 3 Starch, ½ Other Carbohydrate, 5 Very Lean Meat, 2 Fat **Carbohydrate Choices:** 3½

QuickTip

Be sure the turkey thighs are tender before you mix up the dumpling dough. If the dough stands too long the baking powder will start to work and the dumplings may not be as light and fluffy.

prep time
15 minutes

start to finish
6 hours 45 minutes

slow cooker
3½ to 4 quart

4 servings

Turkey-Rotini Casserole

1 cup fat-free chicken broth with 33% less sodium

½ cup water

1 small stalk celery

½ teaspoon dried thyme leaves

1 bay leaf

2 bone-in turkey thighs (about 1½ lb), skin removed

1 package (1.25 oz) Alfredo sauce mix

1 can (10¾ oz) condensed 98% fat-free cream of mushroom soup

1 box (9 oz) frozen cut broccoli, thawed, drained

8 oz uncooked rotini pasta (about 2½ cups)

½ cup grated Parmesan cheese

1. In 3½- to 4-quart slow cooker, mix broth and water. Add celery, thyme and bay leaf. Top with turkey thighs.

2. Cover; cook on Low heat setting 6 to 8 hours.

3. About 35 minutes before serving, remove turkey, celery and bay leaf from slow cooker; discard celery and bay leaf. Increase heat setting to High. In small bowl, mix sauce mix and soup. Stir into liquid in slow cooker. Stir in broccoli. Cover; cook on High heat setting about 30 minutes or until thickened.

4. Meanwhile, cook rotini to desired doneness as directed on package. While rotini is cooking, remove turkey meat from bones and cut into pieces; discard bones. Return turkey to slow cooker. Stir in cooked rotini and cheese.

1 Serving: Calories 560; Total Fat 13g (Saturated Fat 5g; Trans Fat 0g); Cholesterol 120mg; Sodium 1480mg; Total Carbohydrate 63g (Dietary Fiber 5g) **Exchanges:** 3½ Starch, ½ Other Carbohydrate, 5 Very Lean Meat, 1½ Fat **Carbohydrate Choices:** 4

QuickTip

Other shapes of similarly sized pasta work well, too. Try wagon wheels, mafalda (mini lasagna noodles) or penne.

Southwestern Spice–Rubbed Turkey Thighs

2 boneless turkey thighs (about 1½ lb), skin removed

1 tablespoon olive oil

1 teaspoon Cajun seasoning

¼ cup chunky-style salsa

¼ cup sour cream

1. Brush turkey thighs with oil; rub with Cajun seasoning. In 4- to 5-quart slow cooker, place turkey in single layer.

2. Cover; cook on Low heat setting 7 to 8 hours.

3. Just before serving, remove turkey from slow cooker; place on cutting board. Cut turkey into slices. Serve with salsa and sour cream.

1 Serving: Calories 140; Total Fat 8g (Saturated Fat 3g; Trans Fat 0g); Cholesterol 60mg; Sodium 280mg; Total Carbohydrate 2g (Dietary Fiber 0g) **Exchanges:** 2 Lean Meat, ½ Fat **Carbohydrate Choices:** 0

Turkey Drumsticks with Plum Sauce

4 turkey drumsticks (2½ to 3 lb), skin removed

½ teaspoon salt

¼ teaspoon pepper

⅔ cup Chinese plum sauce

⅓ cup sliced green onions

1 tablespoon soy sauce

1 tablespoon cold water

1 tablespoon cornstarch

Hot cooked noodles, if desired

1. Sprinkle turkey drumsticks with salt and pepper. In 5- to 6-quart slow cooker, place drumsticks. In small bowl, mix plum sauce, onions and soy sauce. Pour over turkey.

2. Cover; cook on Low heat setting 8 to 10 hours.

3. About 25 minutes before serving, remove turkey from slow cooker; place on serving platter. Cover with foil to keep warm. Remove any fat from liquid in slow cooker.

4. In small bowl, blend water and cornstarch until smooth. Stir into liquid in slow cooker. Increase heat setting to High. Cover; cook 15 to 20 minutes longer or until sauce has thickened. Remove turkey meat from bones. Serve turkey with sauce over noodles.

1 Serving: Calories 260; Total Fat 6g (Saturated Fat 2g; Trans Fat 0g); Cholesterol 150mg; Sodium 640mg; Total Carbohydrate 13g (Dietary Fiber 0g) **Exchanges:** 1 Other Carbohydrate, 5 Very Lean Meat, ½ Fat **Carbohydrate Choices:** 1

QuickTip

Plum sauce is a sweet-and-sour sauce found in the Asian foods section of your grocery store. If you can't find it, use apricot or cherry preserves with equally delicious results.

Turkey and Wild Rice for Two

½ cup uncooked wild rice, rinsed

½ cup chopped carrot

¼ cup chopped onion

¼ cup thinly sliced celery

½ teaspoon seasoned salt

½ teaspoon garlic-pepper blend

½ teaspoon dried marjoram leaves

1 cup chicken broth

2 tablespoons dry sherry or dry white wine, if desired

1 turkey tenderloin (½ to ¾ lb), cut into ½-inch-thick slices

1. In 1½-quart slow cooker, mix rice, carrot, onion, celery, ¼ teaspoon each of the seasoned salt, garlic-pepper blend and marjoram, the broth and sherry.

2. Arrange turkey slices over rice mixture. Sprinkle with remaining ¼ teaspoon each seasoned salt, garlic-pepper blend and marjoram.

3. Cover; cook on Low heat setting 5 to 6 hours.

1 Serving: Calories 370; Total Fat 8g (Saturated Fat 2g; Trans Fat 0g); Cholesterol 75mg; Sodium 960mg; Total Carbohydrate 41g (Dietary Fiber 4g) **Exchanges:** 2½ Starch, 3½ Very Lean Meat, 1 Fat **Carbohydrate Choices:** 3

Savory Turkey Breast

1 bone-in turkey breast (6 to 6½ lb), thawed if frozen

½ cup chopped onion

½ cup chopped celery

1 bay leaf

1 teaspoon salt

½ teaspoon coarsely ground black pepper

1 teaspoon chicken bouillon granules

½ cup water

1. Remove gravy packet or extra parts from turkey breast; reserve and refrigerate gravy packet if desired. Place onion, celery and bay leaf in cavity of turkey. In 5- to 6-quart slow cooker, place turkey. Sprinkle with salt and pepper.

2. In small bowl, mix bouillon and water until dissolved. Pour over turkey.

3. Cover; cook on Low heat setting 8 to 9 hours.

4. Prepare gravy. Remove turkey from slow cooker; cut into slices. Serve turkey with gravy.

1 Serving: Calories 280; Total Fat 12g (Saturated Fat 3.5g; Trans Fat 0g); Cholesterol 115mg; Sodium 370mg; Total Carbohydrate 0g (Dietary Fiber 0g) **Exchanges:** 6 Very Lean Meat, 1½ Fat **Carbohydrate Choices:** 0

QuickTip

Any leftover turkey can be used to make hot turkey sandwiches. Heat slices of turkey and a jar of gravy until hot. Serve over slices of whole grain bread, and if you like, a side of mashed potatoes.

Turkey and Stuffing with Onion Glaze

1 tablespoon butter or margarine

½ cup chopped onion

1 tablespoon apple jelly

1 package (6 oz) turkey-flavor one-step stuffing mix

¾ cup water

1 boneless skinless turkey breast half (2 to 2½ lb), thawed if frozen

Salt and pepper

1. In 8-inch skillet, melt butter over medium heat. Cook onion in butter 4 to 5 minutes, stirring occasionally, until tender and lightly browned. Stir jelly into onion mixture. Cook 1 to 2 minutes longer, stirring occasionally, until golden brown.

2. Meanwhile, spray 4- to 6-quart slow cooker with cooking spray. Place stuffing mix in slow cooker. Drizzle with water; mix gently. Sprinkle turkey breast half with salt and pepper. Place on stuffing mix. Spoon onion mixture over turkey; spread evenly.

3. Cover; cook on Low heat setting 5 to 6 hours.

4. Cut turkey into slices. Serve stuffing topped with turkey slices.

1 Serving: Calories 350; Total Fat 5g (Saturated Fat 2.5g; Trans Fat 0g); Cholesterol 125mg; Sodium 760mg; Total Carbohydrate 30g (Dietary Fiber 1g) **Exchanges:** 1½ Starch, ½ Other Carbohydrate, 6 Very Lean Meat **Carbohydrate Choices:** 2

Turkey Breast Pot Roast

3 medium red potatoes, cut into 1-inch pieces (about 4 cups)

8 medium carrots, cut into 1-inch pieces (about 2 cups)

1 small onion, cut into wedges (½ cup)

1 bone-in turkey breast with gravy packet (5 to 6 lb), thawed if frozen

1. In 5- to 6-quart slow cooker, mix potatoes, carrots, onion and gravy from turkey breast. Place turkey breast on top of vegetables.

2. Cover; cook on Low heat setting 7 to 8 hours.

3. Remove turkey from slow cooker; cut into slices. Serve turkey with vegetables.

1 Serving: Calories 340; Total Fat 2g (Saturated Fat 0.5g, Trans Fat 0g); Cholesterol 150mg; Sodium 640mg; Total Carbohydrate 23g (Dietary Fiber 3g) **Exchanges:** 1 Starch, 1 Vegetable, 7 Very Lean Meat **Carbohydrate Choices:** 1½

QuickTip

Cranberries are always good with turkey. For an easy cranberry-orange relish, stir the grated peel of a fresh orange (about 1 tablespoon) into 1 can (16 oz) whole berry cranberry sauce.

Turkey and Three-Bean Supper

2 lb ground turkey breast

1 cup finely chopped onions

½ cup molasses

¼ cup cider vinegar

⅛ teaspoon ground cloves

2 cans (28 to 31 oz each) baked beans in tomato sauce, undrained

1 can (19 oz) cannellini beans, drained

1 can (15.5 or 15 oz) kidney beans, drained

Chopped green onions, if desired

1. Spray 10-inch skillet with cooking spray. Heat over medium heat until hot. Add turkey and onion; cook 6 to 8 minutes, stirring frequently, until turkey is no longer pink.

2. Meanwhile, place remaining ingredients except green onions in 3½- to 4-quart slow cooker. Add turkey mixture; mix well.

3. Cover; cook on Low heat setting 6 to 8 hours. Sprinkle individual servings with green onions.

1 Serving: Calories 390; Total Fat 5g (Saturated Fat 1.5g; Trans Fat 0g); Cholesterol 50mg; Sodium 690mg; Total Carbohydrate 56g (Dietary Fiber 10g) **Exchanges:** 3 Starch, ½ Other Carbohydrate, 3 Very Lean Meat **Carbohydrate Choices:** 4

Scalloped Potatoes and Turkey

1 lb ground turkey breast

½ teaspoon ground thyme

⅛ teaspoon pepper

1 box (7.8 oz) scalloped potato mix

2 tablespoons butter or margarine

2½ cups boiling water

1½ cups fat-free (skim) milk

1 medium red bell pepper, seeded, chopped

1 medium onion, thinly sliced

1. Spray 10-inch skillet with cooking spray. Heat over medium-high heat until hot. Add turkey; cook until no longer pink. Stir in thyme and pepper.

2. In large bowl, mix contents of sauce packet from potato mix, potato slices and butter. Add boiling water; stir until butter melts. Add milk; mix well.

3. Stir in turkey, bell pepper and onion. Spoon mixture into 3½- to 4-quart slow cooker. With back of spoon, press down potatoes until covered with sauce.

4. Cover; cook on Low heat setting at least 7 hours.

1 Serving: Calories 310; Total Fat 10g (Saturated Fat 4.5g; Trans Fat 0g); Cholesterol 60mg; Sodium 910mg; Total Carbohydrate 34g (Dietary Fiber 2g) **Exchanges:** 1½ Starch, ½ Other Carbohydrate, 2½ Very Lean Meat, 1½ Fat **Carbohydrate Choices:** 2

Turkey Kielbasa and Sauerkraut Dinner

6 small red potatoes, unpeeled, quartered

8 ready-to-eat baby-cut carrots, cut into ¼-inch slices

1 medium onion, cut into thin wedges

1 tablespoon packed brown sugar

1 tablespoon spicy brown mustard

1 teaspoon caraway seed

1 can (15 oz) sauerkraut

1 lb fully-cooked turkey kielbasa, cut into 1-inch slices

1. In 3½- or 4-quart slow cooker, mix potatoes, carrots and onion.

2. In medium bowl, mix brown sugar, mustard and caraway seed. Stir in sauerkraut and kielbasa. Spoon sauerkraut mixture over vegetables in cooker.

3. Cover; cook on Low heat setting at least 8 hours or until vegetables are tender.

1 Serving: Calories 410; Total Fat 11g (Saturated Fat 3g; Trans Fat 0g); Cholesterol 60mg; Sodium 1750mg; Total Carbohydrate 55g (Dietary Fiber 9g) **Exchanges:** 2 Starch, 1½ Other Carbohydrate, 1 Vegetable, 2 Lean Meat, ½ Fat **Carbohydrate Choices:** 3½

tasty beef
main dishes

Beef Brisket with Cranberry Gravy

2½ lb fresh beef brisket (not corned beef)

½ teaspoon salt

¼ teaspoon pepper

1 can (16 oz) whole berry cranberry sauce

1 can (8 oz) tomato sauce

½ cup chopped onion

1 tablespoon yellow mustard

1. Rub surface of beef brisket with salt and pepper. In 4- to 6-quart slow cooker, place beef. In small bowl, mix remaining ingredients. Pour over beef.

2. Cover; cook on Low heat setting 8 to 10 hours.

3. Remove beef from slow cooker. Cut beef across grain into thin slices. If desired, skim fat from cranberry sauce in slow cooker. Serve beef with sauce.

1 Serving: Calories 300; Total Fat 9g (Saturated Fat 3.5g; Trans Fat 0g); Cholesterol 60mg; Sodium 370mg; Total Carbohydrate 25g (Dietary Fiber 1g) **Exchanges:** ½ Fruit, 1 Other Carbohydrate, 4 Lean Meat **Carbohydrate Choices:** 1½

QuickTip

Whole berry cranberry sauce looks especially pretty in this dish, but you can also use a can of jellied cranberries with equally delicious results.

prep time
15 minutes

start to finish
9 hours 15 minutes

slow cooker
3½ to 4 quart

8 servings

Bavarian Beef Roast with Gravy

3 lb boneless beef rump or tip roast, trimmed of fat

3 tablespoons stone-ground mustard

1 tablespoon creamy horseradish sauce

1 package (0.87 oz) brown gravy mix

½ cup beer or apple juice

½ cup water

3 tablespoons all-purpose flour

1 tablespoon chopped chives

1. In 3½- to 4-quart slow cooker, place beef roast. In small bowl, mix mustard, horseradish sauce and gravy mix. Spread mixture over roast. Pour beer around edge of roast, not on top of roast.

2. Cover; cook on Low heat setting 9 to 10 hours.

3. Remove roast from slow cooker; place on serving platter and cover to keep warm. In 2-quart saucepan, mix water and flour until smooth. Pour cooking juices from slow cooker into saucepan. Heat to boiling over medium-high heat, stirring constantly. Stir in chives. Cut roast into slices; serve with gravy.

1 Serving: Calories 210; Total Fat 6g (Saturated Fat 2g; Trans Fat 0g); Cholesterol 90mg; Sodium 290mg; Total Carbohydrate 0g (Dietary Fiber 0g) Exchanges: 5 Very Lean Meat, ½ Fat Carbohydrate Choices: ½

QuickTip

Coarse stone-ground mustard adds good flavor and texture to this dish, but other mustards can be used, such as spicy brown mustard or country-style Dijon mustard.

Cajun Pot Roast with Maque Choux

2 to 2½ lb boneless beef chuck roast

1 tablespoon Cajun seasoning

1 box (9 oz) frozen whole kernel
    corn

½ cup chopped onion

½ cup chopped green bell pepper

1 can (14.5 oz) diced tomatoes,
    undrained

⅛ teaspoon pepper

½ teaspoon red pepper sauce

1. Rub entire surface of beef roast with Cajun seasoning. In 3½- to 4-quart slow cooker, place roast. Top with frozen corn, onion and bell pepper.

2. In small bowl, mix tomatoes, pepper and pepper sauce. Pour over vegetables and roast.

3. Cover; cook on Low heat setting 8 to 10 hours.

4. To serve, cut roast into slices. Using a slotted spoon, remove corn mixture and serve with roast.

1 Serving: Calories 310; Total Fat 16g (Saturated Fat 6g; Trans Fat 0.5g); Cholesterol 80mg; Sodium 440mg; Total Carbohydrate 12g (Dietary Fiber 2g) **Exchanges:** ½ Other Carbohydrate, 1 Vegetable, 3½ Lean Meat, 1 Fat **Carbohydrate Choices:** 1

QuickTip

Maque choux (pronounced MOCK shoo) means "smothered corn" in Cajun country. This corn is smothered with tomatoes, bell peppers and onions.

Corned Beef and Cabbage

CORNED BEEF

4 medium red potatoes, cut into 1-inch pieces

4 medium carrots, cut into 1-inch pieces

1 medium onion, cut into 6 wedges

2 to 2½ lb corned beef brisket with seasoning packet

1 can (12 oz) beer or nonalcoholic beer

Water

8 thin wedges cabbage

SAUCE

¼ cup applesauce

2 tablespoons Dijon mustard

1. In 4- to 6-quart slow cooker, place potatoes, carrots and onion. Top with corned beef brisket; sprinkle with contents of seasoning packet. Add beer and enough water to just cover corned beef.

2. Cover; cook on Low heat setting 10 to 12 hours.

3. About 30 minutes before serving, remove corned beef from slow cooker; place on serving platter, and cover with foil to keep warm. Add cabbage wedges to vegetables and broth in slow cooker. Increase heat setting to High; cover and cook 30 to 35 minutes longer or until cabbage is crisp-tender.

4. Meanwhile, in small bowl, mix sauce ingredients.

5. To serve, cut corned beef across grain into thin slices. With slotted spoon, remove vegetables from slow cooker. If desired, skim fat from juices in slow cooker. Serve vegetables with juices and corned beef with applesauce-mustard mixture.

1 Serving: Calories 340; Total Fat 16g (Saturated Fat 5g; Trans Fat 0.5g); Cholesterol 80mg; Sodium 1050mg; Total Carbohydrate 30g (Dietary Fiber 5g) **Exchanges:** 1 Starch, ½ Other Carbohydrate, 2 Vegetable, 1½ Medium-Fat Meat, 1½ Fat **Carbohydrate Choices:** 2

QuickTip

If your corned beef doesn't have its own seasoning packet, use ½ teaspoon of black peppercorns, 6 whole cloves and 1 bay leaf. Be sure to remove the bay leaf before serving the juices with the vegetables.

Smothered Swiss Steak

2 teaspoons vegetable oil

1½ lb boneless beef top round steak, trimmed of fat

1 teaspoon salt

¼ teaspoon pepper

1 medium onion, halved lengthwise, thinly sliced

1 carrot, shredded

1 can (4 oz) mushroom pieces and stems, drained

1 can (10¾ oz) condensed cream of mushroom soup

1 can (8 oz) tomato sauce

1. In 10-inch skillet, heat oil over medium-high heat until hot. Cut beef steak into 4 pieces. Place beef in skillet; cook 4 to 6 minutes or until well browned, turning once. Sprinkle beef with salt and pepper.

2. Meanwhile, in 3½- to 4-quart slow cooker, mix onion, carrot and mushrooms.

3. Place beef in slow cooker over vegetables. In same skillet, mix soup and tomato sauce. Pour over beef.

4. Cover; cook on Low heat setting 8 to 10 hours. Stir sauce well before serving over beef.

1 Serving: Calories 330; Total Fat 12g (Saturated Fat 3.5g; Trans Fat 0g); Cholesterol 95mg; Sodium 1590mg; Total Carbohydrate 14g (Dietary Fiber 2g) **Exchanges:** ½ Other Carbohydrate, 1 Vegetable, 5 Lean Meat **Carbohydrate Choices:** 1

Pot-Roasted Steak

1½ lb boneless beef top round steak, 1 inch thick

½ teaspoon paprika

¼ teaspoon pepper

1 cup julienne (matchstick-cut) carrots

1 jar (4.5 oz) sliced mushrooms, undrained

1 can (10¾ oz) condensed cream of mushroom soup

2 tablespoons onion soup mix (from 1-oz package)

1. Spray 3- to 3½-quart slow cooker with cooking spray. Sprinkle beef with paprika and pepper; cut into 4 serving pieces. Place in slow cooker.

2. In medium bowl, mix carrots, mushrooms, soup and dry soup mix; pour over beef.

3. Cover; cook on Low heat setting 5 to 6 hours.

4. Serve steak topped with gravy and vegetables.

1 Serving: Calories 280; Total Fat 10g (Saturated Fat 3g; Trans Fat 0g); Cholesterol 95mg; Sodium 990mg; Total Carbohydrate 12g (Dietary Fiber 2g) **Exchanges:** 1 Starch, 5 Very Lean Meat, 1 Fat **Carbohydrate Choices:** 1

Swiss Steak–Potato Dinner

1½ lb boneless beef round steak, ¾ inch thick, trimmed of fat, cut into 6 serving pieces

½ teaspoon peppered seasoned salt

6 to 8 small red potatoes (about 1¼ lb), cut into quarters

1½ cups ready-to-eat baby-cut carrots

1 medium onion, sliced

1 can (14.5 oz) diced tomatoes with basil, garlic and oregano, undrained

1 jar (12 oz) beef gravy

1. Spray 12-inch skillet with cooking spray. Heat over medium-high heat until hot. Sprinkle beef with peppered seasoned salt; place in skillet. Cook about 8 minutes or until browned, turning once.

2. In 3½- to 6-quart slow cooker, layer potatoes, carrots, beef and onion. In small bowl, mix tomatoes and gravy. Spoon over beef and vegetables.

3. Cover; cook on Low heat setting 7 to 9 hours.

1 Serving: Calories 320; Total Fat 6g (Saturated Fat 2.5g; Trans Fat 0g); Cholesterol 85mg; Sodium 600mg; Total Carbohydrate 27g (Dietary Fiber 4g) **Exchanges:** 1 Starch, 2 Vegetable, 4½ Very Lean Meat, ½ Fat **Carbohydrate Choices:** 2

QuickTip

For a quick family supper, pop some refrigerated baking powder biscuits in the oven and make your favorite bagged crisp green salad.

Mexican Round Steak

1½ lb boneless beef round steak, trimmed of fat, cut into 6 serving pieces

1 cup chopped fresh cilantro

1 cup frozen whole kernel corn, thawed

3 medium stalks celery, thinly sliced (1½ cups)

1 large onion, sliced

½ cup beef broth

1 jar (20 oz) chunky-style salsa

1 can (15 oz) black beans, drained, rinsed

1 cup shredded pepper Jack cheese (4 oz)

1. In 3½- to 6-quart slow cooker, place beef. In medium bowl, mix remaining ingredients except cheese. Pour over beef.

2. Cover; cook on Low heat setting 8 to 9 hours. Sprinkle individual servings with cheese.

1 Serving: Calories 400; Total Fat 10g (Saturated Fat 4.5g; Trans Fat 0g); Cholesterol 100mg; Sodium 850mg; Total Carbohydrate 30g (Dietary Fiber 9g) **Exchanges:** 1½ Starch, 1 Vegetable, 5 Very Lean Meat, 1½ Fat **Carbohydrate Choices:** 2

Green Chile Swiss Steak for Two

2 teaspoons vegetable oil

8 oz boneless beef round steak, trimmed of fat, cut into 2 serving pieces

2 tablespoons taco seasoning mix (from 1.25-oz package)

1 small onion, sliced

¼ cup chopped green chiles (from 4.5-oz can)

½ cup chunky-style salsa

2 tablespoons chili sauce

1. Spray 1½-quart slow cooker with cooking spray. In 10-inch skillet, heat oil over medium-high heat. Cook steak in oil 4 to 5 minutes or until browned on both sides. Sprinkle both sides of steak with 1 tablespoon of the taco seasoning mix.

2. In small bowl, mix remaining 1 tablespoon taco seasoning mix with remaining ingredients. Place 1 steak in bottom of slow cooker. Cover with half of the salsa mixture. Repeat with remaining steak and salsa mixture.

3. Cover; cook on Low heat setting 8 to 9 hours.

1 Serving: Calories 310; Total Fat 10g (Saturated Fat 2.5g; Trans Fat 0g); Cholesterol 85mg; Sodium 1200mg; Total Carbohydrate 19g (Dietary Fiber 4g) **Exchanges:** 1 Other Carbohydrate, 5 Very Lean Meat, 1½ Fat **Carbohydrate Choices:** 1

QuickTip

This is delicious served over hot cooked rice topped with a sprinkle of chopped cilantro. Heat flour tortillas in the microwave to round out the meal.

Beef and Broccoli

1 lb boneless beef top round steak, trimmed of fat, cut into cubes

1 jar (4.5 oz) sliced mushrooms, drained

1 medium onion, cut into wedges

½ cup condensed beef broth

3 tablespoons teriyaki baste and glaze (from 12-oz bottle)

1 tablespoon sesame seed

1 teaspoon dark sesame oil, if desired

⅔ cup uncooked regular long-grain white rice

1⅓ cups water

2 tablespoons water

1 tablespoon cornstarch

2 cups frozen broccoli florets, thawed

1. In 3½- to 4-quart slow cooker, mix beef, mushrooms, onion, broth, teriyaki glaze, sesame seed and sesame oil.

2. Cover; cook on Low heat setting 8 to 10 hours.

3. About 35 minutes before serving, cook rice in 1⅓ cups water as directed on package. Meanwhile, in small bowl, mix 2 tablespoons water and the cornstarch. Stir cornstarch mixture and broccoli into beef mixture. Cover; cook about 30 minutes longer or until broccoli is crisp-tender. Serve over rice.

1 Serving: Calories 340; Total Fat 5g (Saturated Fat 1.5g; Trans Fat 0g); Cholesterol 60mg; Sodium 640mg; Total Carbohydrate 41g (Dietary Fiber 4g) **Exchanges:** 1½ Starch, 1 Other Carbohydrate, 1 Vegetable, 3½ Very Lean Meat, ½ Fat **Carbohydrate Choices:** 3

QuickTip

Dark sesame oil has a much stronger flavor than light-colored sesame oil. It's used as an accent oil, to give a boost of aroma and flavor to a finished dish.

Teriyaki Beef and Vegetables

1½ lb beef round steak, trimmed of fat, cut into thin bite-sized strips

2 tablespoons cornstarch

¼ cup soy sauce

¼ cup dry sherry or apple juice

2 tablespoons packed brown sugar

1 teaspoon ground ginger

1 clove garlic, finely chopped

1 can (8 oz) sliced water chestnuts, drained

¼ cup water

1 bag (1 lb) frozen broccoli, carrots & cauliflower, thawed*

1½ cups uncooked regular long-grain white rice

3 cups water

1. In 4- to 5-quart slow cooker, mix steak and 1 tablespoon of the cornstarch until evenly coated. Gently stir in soy sauce, sherry, brown sugar, ginger and garlic. Top with water chestnuts.

2. Cover; cook on Low heat setting about 6 hours.

3. About 30 minutes before serving, in small bowl, blend ¼ cup water and remaining 1 tablespoon cornstarch until smooth. Stir into beef mixture. Stir in thawed vegetables.

4. Increase heat setting to High; cover and cook 25 to 30 minutes longer or until vegetables are crisp-tender. Meanwhile, cook rice in 3 cups water as directed on package. Serve beef mixture over rice.

*To thaw frozen vegetables, place in colander or strainer; rinse with warm water until thawed. Drain well.

1 Serving: Calories 440; Total Fat 5g (Saturated Fat 1.5g; Trans Fat 0g); Cholesterol 85mg; Sodium 670mg; Total Carbohydrate 56g (Dietary Fiber 3g) Exchanges: 2½ Starch, 1 Other Carbohydrate, 1 Vegetable, 4½ Very Lean Meat Carbohydrate Choices: 4

Swiss Steak with Chipotle Chile Sauce

1 can (10¾ oz) condensed cream of mushroom soup

2 lb boneless beef top round steak, 1½ inches thick

1 tablespoon packed brown sugar

2 tablespoons ketchup

2 tablespoons chopped chipotle chiles in adobo sauce (from 7- or 11-oz can)

1 clove garlic, finely chopped

2 medium plum (Roma) tomatoes, chopped

½ medium green bell pepper, cut into thin bite-sized strips

1. Spoon soup into 4- to 5-quart slow cooker. Top with beef round steak, cutting into pieces if necessary to place in single layer. In small bowl, mix brown sugar, ketchup, chiles and garlic. Spread over beef. Top with tomatoes.

2. Cover; cook on Low heat setting 8 to 9 hours.

3. Add bell pepper. Cover; cook 10 minutes longer.

4. To serve, remove beef from slow cooker; cut into serving-sized pieces. Serve beef with sauce from slow cooker.

1 Serving: Calories 180; Total Fat 6g (Saturated Fat 2g; Trans Fat 0g); Cholesterol 65mg; Sodium 360mg; Total Carbohydrate 7g (Dietary Fiber 0g) Exchanges: ½ Other Carbohydrate, 3½ Very Lean Meat, 1 Fat Carbohydrate Choices: ½

Rosemary Beef with Noodles

2 tablespoons butter or margarine, melted

1 tablespoon dried minced onion

1 teaspoon beef base (from a jar)

½ teaspoon salt

¼ teaspoon pepper

1½ lb beef stew meat, cut into 1½-inch cubes

4½ cups uncooked wide egg noodles (8 oz)

4 plum (Roma) tomatoes, chopped

1 teaspoon chopped fresh rosemary leaves

1. In 4- to 6-quart slow cooker, mix melted butter, dried minced onion, beef base, salt, pepper and beef.

2. Cover; cook on Low heat setting 9 to 10 hours.

3. About 15 minutes before serving, cook and drain noodles as directed on package. Meanwhile, add tomatoes and rosemary to beef mixture; mix well. Increase heat setting to High. Cover; cook 10 minutes longer. Serve beef mixture over noodles.

1 Serving: Calories 550; Total Fat 27g (Saturated Fat 11g; Trans Fat 1g); Cholesterol 145mg; Sodium 940mg; Total Carbohydrate 41g (Dietary Fiber 2g) **Exchanges:** 2 Starch, ½ Other Carbohydrate, 4 Lean Meat, 3 Fat Carbohydrate Choices: 3

QuickTip

If you prefer, use 1 cup chopped onion in place of the dried minced onion.

Beef Stroganoff with Rice

1½ lb boneless beef round steak, trimmed of fat, cut into bite-sized strips

2 tablespoons onion soup mix (from 1-oz package)

1 jar (4.5 oz) sliced mushrooms, drained

1 can (10¾ oz) condensed cream of mushroom soup

1½ cups uncooked regular long-grain white rice

3 cups water

½ cup sour cream

2 tablespoons chopped fresh chives

1. In 2- to 3-quart slow cooker, mix beef strips and dry soup mix until evenly coated. Top with mushrooms and soup.

2. Cover; cook on Low heat setting 7 to 8 hours.

3. About 30 minutes before serving, cook rice in water as directed on package. Just before serving, stir sour cream into beef mixture. Serve over rice; sprinkle with chives.

1 Serving: Calories 410; Total Fat 11g (Saturated Fat 4.5g; Trans Fat 0g); Cholesterol 80mg; Sodium 1220mg; Total Carbohydrate 47g (Dietary Fiber 1g) **Exchanges:** 3 Starch, 3 Very Lean Meat, 1½ Fat **Carbohydrate Choices:** 3

Saucy Short Ribs

3½ to 4 lb beef short ribs, cut into pieces

½ teaspoon seasoned salt

¼ teaspoon pepper

1 medium onion, cut into thin wedges

1 can (10¾ oz) condensed cream of celery soup

½ cup chili sauce

1 tablespoon Worcestershire sauce

1. Sprinkle beef ribs with seasoned salt and pepper. In 3½- to 4-quart slow cooker, layer ribs and onion. In small bowl, mix remaining ingredients. Pour over ribs.

2. Cover; cook on Low heat setting 7 to 9 hours. Remove excess fat from top of sauce; serve sauce over ribs.

1 Serving: Calories 270; Total Fat 17g (Saturated Fat 6g; Trans Fat 1g); Cholesterol 75mg; Sodium 850mg; Total Carbohydrate 11g (Dietary Fiber 2g) **Exchanges:** ½ Other Carbohydrate, 3 Medium-Fat Meat, ½ Fat **Carbohydrate Choices:** 1

Cheesy Italian Tortellini

½ lb lean (at least 80%) ground beef

½ lb bulk Italian pork sausage

1 cup sliced fresh mushrooms

1 container (15 oz) refrigerated marinara sauce

1 can (14.5 oz) diced tomatoes with Italian seasoning, undrained

1 package (9 oz) refrigerated cheese-filled tortellini

1 cup shredded mozzarella cheese or pizza cheese blend (4 oz)

1. In 10-inch skillet, break beef and sausage into large pieces. Cook over medium heat about 10 minutes, stirring occasionally, until browned.

2. Spray 4- to 5-quart slow cooker with cooking spray. In slow cooker, mix meat mixture, mushrooms, marinara sauce and tomatoes.

3. Cover; cook on Low heat setting 7 to 8 hours.

4. About 15 minutes before serving, add tortellini to slow cooker; stir gently to mix. Sprinkle with cheese. Cover; cook about 15 minutes longer or until tortellini are tender.

1 Serving: Calories 610; Total Fat 28g (Saturated Fat 11g; Trans Fat 0.5g); Cholesterol 95mg; Sodium 1260mg; Total Carbohydrate 55g (Dietary Fiber 4g) **Exchanges:** 1½ Starch, 2 Other Carbohydrate, 1 Vegetable, 3½ High-Fat Meat **Carbohydrate Choices:** 0½

QuickTip

If you don't have a can of the diced tomatoes with Italian seasoning, substitute a can of plain diced tomatoes and ½ teaspoon Italian seasoning.

Cheesy Ravioli Casserole

1 tablespoon olive or vegetable oil

1 medium onion, chopped (½ cup)

1 large clove garlic, finely chopped

2 jars (26 oz each) four cheese–flavored tomato pasta sauce

1 can (15 oz) tomato sauce

1 teaspoon Italian seasoning

2 packages (25 oz each) frozen beef-filled ravioli

2 cups shredded mozzarella cheese (8 oz)

¼ cup chopped fresh parsley

1. Spray 5- to 6-quart slow cooker with cooking spray. In Dutch oven or 12-inch skillet, heat oil over medium heat until hot. Cook onion and garlic in oil about 4 minutes, stirring occasionally, until onion is tender. Stir in pasta sauce, tomato sauce and Italian seasoning.

2. Place 1 cup of the sauce mixture in slow cooker. Add 1 package frozen ravioli; top with 1 cup of the cheese. Top with remaining package of ravioli and 1 cup cheese. Pour remaining sauce mixture over top.

3. Cover; cook on Low heat setting 5½ to 6½ hours or until hot. Sprinkle with parsley before serving.

1 Serving: Calories 500; Total Fat 17g (Saturated Fat 7g; Trans Fat 0g); Cholesterol 40mg; Sodium 1380mg; Total Carbohydrate 65g (Dietary Fiber 4g) **Exchanges:** 2½ Starch, 1½ Other Carbohydrate, 1 Vegetable, 2 Medium-Fat Meat, 1 Fat **Carbohydrate Choices:** 4

QuickTip

To easily chop parsley, trim the stems and place the leaves in a 1-cup glass measuring cup. Use kitchen scissors to snip the leaves, rotating the cup until all the parsley is chopped.

Beef Burgundy

1½ cups ready-to-eat baby-cut carrots, cut in half crosswise

2 lb cubed beef stew meat

1 cup frozen small whole onions (from 1-lb bag)

1 package (8 oz) fresh small whole mushrooms

1 clove garlic, finely chopped

1 teaspoon salt

¼ teaspoon pepper

1 dried bay leaf

½ cup red Burgundy wine

1 can (10½ oz) condensed beef consommé

2 tablespoons all-purpose flour

2 tablespoons water

1. Spray 4- to 5-quart slow cooker with cooking spray. In cooker, layer all ingredients except flour and water in order listed.

2. Cover; cook on Low heat setting 10 to 12 hours.

3. About 35 minutes before serving, remove and discard bay leaf. In small bowl, mix flour and water until smooth. Gradually stir flour mixture into beef mixture.

4. Increase heat setting to High. Cover; cook 15 to 30 minutes longer or until slightly thickened.

1 Serving: Calories 400; Total Fat 21g (Saturated Fat 8g, Trans Fat 1g); Cholesterol 110mg; Sodium 890mg; Total Carbohydrate 11g (Dietary Fiber 2g) Exchanges: ½ Starch, 1 Vegetable, 5½ Lean Meat, 1 Fat Carbohydrate Choices: 1

QuickTip

When cleaning fresh mushrooms, dampen them slightly and clean with a stiff brush or damp towel. Avoid soaking fresh mushrooms in water because they are sponge-like and will absorb water, resulting in a final dish with too much liquid.

Beef and Bean Tamale Pie

½ lb lean (at least 80%) ground beef

½ cup chopped onion

1 can (15 or 15.5 oz) kidney beans, drained, rinsed

1 can (10 oz) enchilada sauce

1 pouch (6.5 oz) cornbread and muffin mix

⅓ cup milk

2 tablespoons butter or margarine, melted

1 egg

½ cup shredded Colby-Monterey Jack cheese blend (2 oz)

1 can (4.5 oz) chopped green chiles

¼ cup sour cream

4 medium green onions, chopped (¼ cup)

1. In 10-inch skillet, cook beef and onion over medium heat 8 to 10 minutes, stirring occasionally, until beef is thoroughly cooked; drain. Stir in beans and enchilada sauce. In 3½- to 4½-quart slow cooker, place beef mixture.

2. In small bowl, mix cornbread mix, milk, melted butter and egg; stir just until moistened. (Batter will be lumpy.) Add cheese and chiles; stir gently to mix. Spoon over beef mixture in slow cooker.

3. Cover; cook on Low heat setting 5 to 6 hours or until toothpick inserted in center of cornbread comes out clean. Top individual servings with sour cream and onions.

1 Serving: Calories 590; Total Fat 23g (Saturated Fat 11g; Trans Fat 1g); Cholesterol 130mg; Sodium 1030mg; Total Carbohydrate 67g (Dietary Fiber 8g) **Exchanges:** 2½ Starch, 2 Other Carbohydrate, 3 Medium-Fat Meat, 1 Fat **Carbohydrate Choices:** 4½

busy-day pork & sausage

Cranberry-Onion Pork Roast

2½ to 3 lb boneless pork shoulder roast, trimmed of fat

1 can (16 oz) whole berry cranberry sauce

1 package (1 oz) onion soup mix (from 2-oz box)

1. In 3- to 4-quart slow cooker, place roast. In small bowl, mix cranberry sauce and soup mix; spread over roast.

2. Cover; cook on Low heat setting 8 to 9 hours or until pork is tender.

3. Remove pork and cut into slices; serve with sauce.

1 Serving: Calories 350; Total Fat 19g (Saturated Fat 7g; Trans Fat 0g); Cholesterol 85mg; Sodium 340mg; Total Carbohydrate 22g (Dietary Fiber 0g) **Exchanges:** 1½ Other Carbohydrate, 3½ Lean Meat, 1½ Fat **Carbohydrate Choices:** 1½

QuickTip

Whole berry cranberry sauce makes a prettier sauce but jellied cranberry sauce can be used. Serve broccoli spears and bread stuffing for an easy, tasty meal.

prep time
15 minutes

start to finish
7 hours 15 minutes

slow cooker
5 to 6 quart

6 servings

Pork Roast and Sauerkraut Dinner

PORK ROAST DINNER

1 package (32 oz) refrigerated sauerkraut, drained

2 medium apples, peeled, sliced

1 teaspoon caraway seed

¼ cup apple juice or water

1 boneless pork roast (2½ to 3 lb), string removed, trimmed of fat

6 small red potatoes (about 18 oz), cut in half

1 tablespoon Dijon mustard

MUSTARD SAUCE

3 tablespoons Dijon mustard

2 tablespoons packed brown sugar

1. In 5- to 6-quart slow cooker, lightly mix sauerkraut, apples, caraway seed and apple juice. With spoon, make indention in center of mixture; place pork roast in center.

2. Arrange potato halves around roast on sauerkraut mixture. Spread 1 tablespoon mustard over pork.

3. Cover; cook on Low heat setting 7 to 8 hours.

4. In small bowl, mix sauce ingredients. Remove pork from slow cooker; cut into slices. Arrange pork and potatoes on serving platter. With slotted spoon, remove sauerkraut mixture from slow cooker; place in serving bowl. Serve pork and potatoes with sauerkraut mixture and mustard sauce.

1 Serving: Calories 330; Total Fat 10g (Saturated Fat 3g; Trans Fat 0g); Cholesterol 70mg; Sodium 1170mg; Total Carbohydrate 33g (Dietary Fiber 6g) **Exchanges:** 1 Starch, 1 Other Carbohydrate, 1 Vegetable, 3 Lean Meat **Carbohydrate Choices:** 2

QuickTip

It's best not to rinse the sauerkraut, as it will dilute the unique flavor that sauerkraut gives this recipe.

prep time
15 minutes

start to finish
8 hours 15 minutes

slow cooker
3½ to 4 quart

6 servings

Autumn Pork Roast Dinner

1¾ to 2 lb rolled boneless pork loin roast

¼ teaspoon salt

⅛ teaspoon pepper

3 large dark-orange sweet potatoes, peeled, thinly sliced

1 medium onion, sliced, separated into rings

¾ teaspoon dried thyme leaves

1 quart apple juice (4 cups)

1. Sprinkle pork roast with salt and pepper. In 3½- to 4-quart slow cooker, place pork. Place sliced sweet potatoes around and on top of pork. Top with onion. Sprinkle with thyme. Pour apple juice over onion.

2. Cover; cook on Low heat setting at least 8 hours or until pork is tender. Remove pork and cut into slices. Using a slotted spoon, remove the potatoes and onions; serve with the pork.

1 Serving: Calories 370; Total Fat 11g (Saturated Fat 3.5g; Trans Fat 0g); Cholesterol 85mg; Sodium 180mg; Total Carbohydrate 37g (Dietary Fiber 3g) **Exchanges:** 1 Starch, 1 Fruit, ½ Other Carbohydrate, 4 Lean Meat **Carbohydrate Choices:** 2½

Cranberry-Orange Pork Roast

2½ lb boneless pork shoulder roast, trimmed of fat

1 cup sweetened dried cranberries

½ cup chicken broth

1 teaspoon shredded orange peel

½ cup cranberry juice cocktail

2 tablespoons cornstarch

1. In 3½- to 4-quart slow cooker, place pork roast. In small bowl, mix cranberries, broth, orange peel and ¼ cup of the cranberry juice cocktail. Pour over pork.

2. Cover; cook on Low heat setting 7 to 9 hours.

3. Remove pork from slow cooker; place on serving platter. Cover with foil. Pour juices from slow cooker into 2-quart saucepan; if necessary, skim off any fat.

4. In small bowl, mix remaining ¼ cup cranberry juice cocktail and cornstarch until smooth. Stir into juices in saucepan. Cook over medium heat, stirring constantly, until bubbly and thickened. Cut pork into slices. Serve pork with sauce.

1 Serving: Calories 460; Total Fat 23g (Saturated Fat 8g; Trans Fat 0g); Cholesterol 120mg; Sodium 160mg; Total Carbohydrate 22g (Dietary Fiber 1g) **Exchanges:** 1½ Other Carbohydrate, 5½ Lean Meat, 1½ Fat **Carbohydrate Choices:** 1½

QuickTip

This easy and elegant dish is perfect served with whole green beans and mixed-rice pilaf. Add some fresh-baked refrigerated crescent rolls, and you'll win rave reviews.

prep time
15 minutes

start to finish
8 hours 15 minutes

slow cooker
3½ to 4 quart

6 servings

Porketta with Two Potatoes

2 medium dark-orange sweet potatoes, peeled, cut into ½-inch cubes (about 2½ cups)

2 medium Yukon Gold potatoes, cut into ½-inch cubes (about 2½ cups)

2 teaspoons fennel seed, crushed

1 teaspoon dried oregano leaves

1 teaspoon paprika

½ teaspoon garlic powder

½ teaspoon salt

¼ teaspoon pepper

2 lb boneless pork loin roast

1 cup chicken broth

1. In 3½- to 4-quart slow cooker, place potatoes. In small bowl, mix fennel seed, oregano, paprika, garlic powder, salt and pepper. Rub into pork roast. Place pork on potatoes. Pour broth over pork and potatoes.

2. Cover; cook on Low heat setting 8 to 10 hours.

3. Remove pork and cut into slices. Serve with potatoes.

1 Serving: Calories 280; Total Fat 9g (Saturated Fat 3g; Trans Fat 0g); Cholesterol 70mg; Sodium 430mg; Total Carbohydrate 22g (Dietary Fiber 3g) **Exchanges:** 1½ Starch, 3 Lean Meat **Carbohydrate Choices:** 1½

QuickTip

Rubbing the pork roast with the seasoning mixture the night before and refrigerating it does double duty. It saves time in the morning and it allows the seasonings to flavor the pork.

Barbecued Pork Chops for Two

2 boneless pork loin chops,
    1 inch thick (about ¾ lb),
    trimmed of fat

2 slices onion

1 clove garlic, finely chopped

½ cup barbecue sauce

1 tablespoon water

1 teaspoon cornstarch

1. In 2- to 3½-quart slow cooker, place pork chops. Top each with onion slice; sprinkle with garlic. Pour barbecue sauce over pork.

2. Cover; cook on Low heat setting 5 to 6 hours.

3. About 5 minutes before serving, remove pork from slow cooker; place on serving platter. Top each chop with onion slice; cover to keep warm.

4. In 2-cup glass measuring cup or small microwavable bowl, mix water and cornstarch until smooth. Stir juices from slow cooker into cornstarch mixture. Microwave uncovered on High 1 to 2 minutes, stirring once halfway through cooking, until mixture boils and thickens slightly. Serve sauce with pork.

1 Serving: Calories 380; Total Fat 13g (Saturated Fat 4.5g; Trans Fat 0g); Cholesterol 105mg; Sodium 720mg; Total Carbohydrate 29g (Dietary Fiber 0g) **Exchanges:** 2 Other Carbohydrate, 5 Lean Meat **Carbohydrate Choices:** 2

Pizza Pork Chops

6 pork loin chops, 1 inch thick
   (6 oz each)

½ teaspoon salt

¼ teaspoon pepper

1 tablespoon vegetable oil

1 medium onion, chopped (½ cup)

2 cups tomato pasta sauce

1 cup shredded mozzarella cheese
   (4 oz)

1. Sprinkle pork chops with salt and pepper. In 12-inch skillet, heat oil over medium-high heat until hot. Add pork; cook about 5 minutes or until browned, turning once.

2. In 3½- to 6-quart slow cooker, place pork. Sprinkle onion over pork. Pour pasta sauce over top.

3. Cover; cook on Low heat setting 4 to 6 hours.

4. Place pork on serving platter. Top with sauce. Sprinkle with cheese.

1 Serving: Calories 370; Total Fat 18g (Saturated Fat 6g; Trans Fat 0g); Cholesterol 85mg; Sodium 750mg; Total Carbohydrate 18g (Dietary Fiber 1g) **Exchanges:** 1 Other Carbohydrate, 4½ Lean Meat, 1 Fat **Carbohydrate Choices:** 1

QuickTip

For a flavor change, use a tomato pasta sauce with mushrooms or roasted garlic and herbs; try shredded Parmesan cheese on top rather than mozzarella cheese.

Pork Chops with Spiced Fruit Stuffing

1 cup diced dried fruit and raisin mixture

1 cup chicken broth

½ cup apple juice

3 tablespoons butter or margarine

¼ teaspoon ground cinnamon

⅛ teaspoon ground nutmeg

1 package (6 oz) herb-seasoned one-step stuffing mix

4 boneless pork loin chops, ½ inch thick (4 oz each)

⅛ teaspoon salt

⅛ teaspoon pepper

1. In 4-quart saucepan, mix dried fruits, broth, ¼ cup of the apple juice, the butter, cinnamon and nutmeg. Heat to boiling. Stir in stuffing mix. Remove from heat.

2. In bottom of 3½- or 4-quart slow cooker, arrange pork chops. Pour remaining ¼ cup apple juice over pork. Sprinkle with salt and pepper. Top with stuffing mixture.

3. Cover; cook on Low heat setting 5 to 6 hours.

4. Place stuffing in serving bowl. Stir gently. Serve pork with stuffing.

1 Serving: Calories 530; Total Fat 19g (Saturated Fat 9g; Trans Fat 0.5g); Cholesterol 95mg; Sodium 1120mg; Total Carbohydrate 58g (Dietary Fiber 4g) **Exchanges:** 2 Starch, 1 Fruit, 1 Other Carbohydrate, 3½ Lean Meat, 1½ Fat **Carbohydrate Choices:** 4

QuickTip

If you don't have diced dried fruit and raisin mixture on hand, use one cup raisins or dried cranberries.

Sweet-and-Sour Pork

1½ lb boneless pork loin, cut into cubes

1 can (8 oz) pineapple tidbits in unsweetened juice, undrained

1 medium red or green bell pepper, cut into squares

3 tablespoons brown sugar

½ teaspoon ginger

¼ cup vinegar

3 tablespoons soy sauce

⅔ cup uncooked regular long-grain white rice

1⅓ cups water

3 tablespoons water

2 tablespoons cornstarch

1. In 3½- to 4-quart slow cooker, combine pork, pineapple, bell pepper, brown sugar, ginger, vinegar and soy sauce; mix well.

2. Cover; cook on low setting for 6 to 8 hours.

3. About 25 minutes before serving, cook rice in 1⅓ cups water as directed on package.

4. About 5 minutes before serving, in small bowl, combine 3 tablespoons water and cornstarch; blend well. Stir into pork mixture in slow cooker. Cover; cook on high setting for an additional 5 minutes or until thickened. Serve pork mixture over rice.

1 Serving: Calories 500; Total Fat 14g (Saturated Fat 4.5g; Trans Fat 0g); Cholesterol 110mg; Sodium 1110mg; Total Carbohydrate 52g (Dietary Fiber 1g) **Exchanges:** 2 Starch, 1½ Other Carbohydrate, 4½ Lean Meat **Carbohydrate Choices:** 3½

Teriyaki Pork Ribs for Two

¾ to 1 lb boneless country-style pork ribs

½ teaspoon garlic-pepper blend

¼ teaspoon ground ginger

¼ cup teriyaki baste and glaze

2 tablespoons chili sauce or ketchup

2 tablespoons pineapple preserves

1. Spray 1½-quart slow cooker with cooking spray. Trim fat from ribs and cut in half to fit slow cooker. Sprinkle ribs with garlic-pepper blend and ginger; place in slow cooker.

2. In small bowl, mix remaining ingredients; pour over ribs.

3. Cover; cook on Low heat setting 7 to 8 hours.

4. Remove ribs from slow cooker. Skim off and discard fat from surface of liquid in slow cooker. Stir mixture well; serve with ribs.

1 Serving: Calories 300; Total Fat 11g (Saturated Fat 4g; Trans Fat 0g); Cholesterol 60mg; Sodium 1080mg; Total Carbohydrate 29g (Dietary Fiber 1g) Exchanges: 2 Other Carbohydrate, 3 Lean Meat, ½ Fat Carbohydrate Choices: 2

QuickTip

If you've purchased country-style ribs with bones (instead of boneless), you'll need 1 to 1¼ pounds to make this dish. Cut them into sections to fit them into the slow cooker.

Polynesian Pork Ribs

RIBS

2 lb boneless country-style pork loin ribs

1 clove garlic, finely chopped

1 small onion, sliced

1 can (8 oz) crushed pineapple in juice, undrained

SAUCE

¾ cup ketchup

3 tablespoons packed brown sugar

3 tablespoons hoisin sauce

1 teaspoon grated gingerroot

Hot cooked rice, if desired

1. Spray 3½- to 4-quart slow cooker with cooking spray. Place pork ribs, garlic and onion in slow cooker. Spoon about half of the pineapple with some of the juice over ribs. Reserve remaining pineapple and juice.

2. Cover; cook on Low heat setting 8 to 10 hours.

3. About 35 minutes before serving, drain and discard cooking juices from slow cooker; wipe edge of slow cooker clean. In small bowl, mix ketchup, brown sugar, hoisin sauce, gingerroot and remaining pineapple with juice. Spoon or pour evenly over ribs. Increase heat setting to High. Cover; cook 25 to 30 minutes longer or until ribs are glazed. Serve with rice.

1 Serving: Calories 390; Total Fat 22g (Saturated Fat 8g; Trans Fat 0g); Cholesterol 90mg; Sodium 530mg; Total Carbohydrate 25g (Dietary Fiber 1g) **Exchanges:** 1½ Other Carbohydrate, 3 Lean Meat, 3 Fat **Carbohydrate Choices:** 1½

QuickTip

If you don't have fresh gingerroot on hand, use ¼ teaspoon of ground ginger instead.

prep time
15 minutes

start to finish
7 hours 15 minutes

slow cooker
3½ to 4 quart

4 servings

Key West Ribs

2½ lb country-style pork loin ribs

¼ cup finely chopped onion

¼ cup barbecue sauce

1 teaspoon grated lime peel

2 tablespoons lime juice

1 teaspoon grated orange peel

¼ cup orange juice

½ teaspoon salt

1. In 3½- to 4-quart slow cooker, place pork ribs. In small bowl, mix remaining ingredients. Pour over ribs.

2. Cover; cook on Low heat setting 7 to 9 hours. Spoon sauce over ribs.

1 Serving: Calories 570; Total Fat 41g (Saturated Fat 15g; Trans Fat 0g); Cholesterol 165mg; Sodium 590mg; Total Carbohydrate 10g (Dietary Fiber 0g) **Exchanges:** ½ Other Carbohydrate, 5½ High-Fat Meat **Carbohydrate Choices:** ½

prep time
10 minutes

start to finish
8 hours 15 minutes

slow cooker
3 to 4 quart

6 servings

Santa Fe Country Ribs

2 lb boneless country-style pork
   ribs

½ teaspoon salt

¾ cup chunky-style salsa

¾ cup chili sauce

1 teaspoon ground cumin

¼ teaspoon ground red pepper
   (cayenne)

2 tablespoons tomato paste (from
   6-oz can)

1. Spray 3- to 4-quart slow cooker with cooking spray. Place pork ribs in slow cooker; sprinkle with salt. In small bowl, mix salsa, chili sauce, cumin and ground red pepper; spoon over ribs.

2. Cover; cook on Low heat setting 8 to 9 hours.

3. Remove ribs from slow cooker; place on serving platter. Into 2-cup measuring cup or bowl, pour 1 cup cooking juices from slow cooker. Stir in tomato paste; spoon over ribs.

1 Serving: Calories 210; Total Fat 10g (Saturated Fat 3.5g; Trans Fat 0g); Cholesterol 50mg; Sodium 920mg; Total Carbohydrate 10g (Dietary Fiber 3g) **Exchanges:** ½ Other Carbohydrate, 2½ Medium-Fat Meat **Carbohydrate Choices:** ½

QuickTip

Leftover tomato paste can be easily frozen by dropping onto waxed paper in two-tablespoon quantities and freezing until firm. Transfer to a freezer plastic bag. Add one portion to vegetable, rice or pasta mixtures for a rich tomato flavor.

Country-Style Ribs and Sauerkraut

2 lb boneless country-style pork loin ribs

1 medium cooking apple, sliced

1 small onion, sliced

1 can (16 oz) sauerkraut, drained, rinsed

3 tablespoons packed brown sugar

1 teaspoon caraway seed

¼ cup dry white wine or apple juice

1. In 3½- or 4-quart slow cooker, place pork ribs, apple and onion. Top with sauerkraut, brown sugar and caraway seed; mix lightly. Pour wine over top.

2. Cover; cook on Low heat setting 8 to 10 hours.

1 Serving: Calories 220; Total Fat 10g (Saturated Fat 3.5g; Trans Fat 0g); Cholesterol 50mg; Sodium 440mg; Total Carbohydrate 14g (Dietary Fiber 2g) **Exchanges:** 1 Other Carbohydrate, 2½ Lean Meat, ½ Fat **Carbohydrate Choices:** 1

Slow-and-Easy Barbecued Ribs

2 lb boneless country-style pork loin ribs

1 medium onion, sliced

1 clove garlic, finely chopped

⅔ cup barbecue sauce

⅓ cup plum jam

1. Spray 4- to 6-quart slow cooker with cooking spray. Place pork ribs, onion and garlic in slow cooker.

2. Cover; cook on Low heat setting 8 to 10 hours.

3. About 35 minutes before serving, drain and discard juices from slow cooker; wipe edge of cooker clean. In measuring cup, mix barbecue sauce and jam. Pour or spoon mixture over ribs, coating evenly.

4. Increase heat setting to High. Cover; cook 25 to 30 minutes longer or until ribs are glazed. Serve ribs with sauce.

1 Serving: Calories 390; Total Fat 22g (Saturated Fat 8g; Trans Fat 0g); Cholesterol 90mg; Sodium 370mg; Total Carbohydrate 26g (Dietary Fiber 0g) **Exchanges:** 1½ Other Carbohydrate, 3 High-Fat Meat **Carbohydrate Choices:** 2

QuickTip

Plum jam adds a subtle sweetness to these barbecued ribs. If you don't have plum jam, use ⅓ cup grape jelly or jam.

prep time
15 minutes

start to finish
6 hours 15 minutes

slow cooker
4 to 6 quart

12 servings

Honey-Dijon Ham

5 lb cooked bone-in ham

⅓ cup apple juice

¼ cup packed brown sugar

1 tablespoon honey

1 tablespoon Dijon mustard

1. In 4- to 6-quart slow cooker, place ham. Add apple juice. In small bowl, mix brown sugar, honey and mustard. Spread mixture over ham.

2. Cover; cook on Low heat setting 6 to 8 hours.

3. Remove ham and cut into slices.

1 Serving: Calories 150; Total Fat 5g (Saturated Fat 1.5g; Trans Fat 0g); Cholesterol 50mg; Sodium 1130mg; Total Carbohydrate 8g (Dietary Fiber 0g) Exchanges: ½ Other Carbohydrate, 2½ Lean Meat Carbohydrate Choices: ½

QuickTip

If the whole ham is too large for your slow cooker, cut it in half and fit the two pieces side by side.

prep time
15 minutes

start to finish
6 hours 15 minutes

slow cooker
3½ to 4 quart

6 servings

Bolognese Sauce with Spaghetti

6 Italian sausage links (about 1½ lb), cut into 1-inch pieces

1 cup finely chopped onions (1 large)

3 tablespoons sugar

1 teaspoon dried basil leaves

1 teaspoon dried oregano leaves

½ teaspoon salt

2 cloves garlic, finely chopped

1 can (28 oz) crushed tomatoes, undrained

1 can (15 oz) tomato sauce

1 can (12 oz) tomato paste

12 oz uncooked spaghetti

1. In 3½- to 4-quart slow cooker, mix all ingredients except spaghetti.

2. Cover; cook on Low heat setting 6 to 8 hours. Skim and discard fat, if desired.

3. About 30 minutes before serving, cook spaghetti to desired doneness as directed on package. Serve sauce over spaghetti.

1 Serving: Calories 670; Total Fat 25g (Saturated Fat 8g; Trans Fat 0g); Cholesterol 45mg; Sodium 2430mg; Total Carbohydrate 82g (Dietary Fiber 8g) **Exchanges:** 2½ Starch, 2 Other Carbohydrate, 2½ Vegetable, 2½ High-Fat Meat, ½ Fat **Carbohydrate Choices:** 5½

QuickTip

If you have Italian seasoning in your spice rack, use two teaspoons for the basil and oregano.

Pineapple-Orange Glazed Ham

3 lb cooked boneless ham

1 can (8 oz) crushed pineapple in juice

½ cup packed brown sugar

3 tablespoons orange marmalade

1 teaspoon yellow mustard

1. In 3½- to 5-quart slow cooker, place ham. Drain pineapple juice from can into slow cooker; refrigerate pineapple. In small bowl, mix brown sugar, 1 tablespoon of the marmalade and the mustard. Spread over ham.

2. Cover; cook on Low heat setting 6 to 8 hours.

3. About 5 minutes before serving, in small microwavable bowl, mix pineapple and remaining 2 tablespoons orange marmalade. Microwave uncovered on High 1¼ to 1½ minutes or until hot, stirring once halfway through cooking.

4. Remove ham and cut into slices. Serve with pineapple mixture.

1 Serving: Calories 310; Total Fat 12g (Saturated Fat 4.5g; Trans Fat 0g); Cholesterol 80mg; Sodium 2050mg; Total Carbohydrate 18g (Dietary Fiber 0g) **Exchanges:** 1 Other Carbohydrate, 4½ Very Lean Meat, 2 Fat **Carbohydrate Choices:** 1

Ham and Scalloped Potatoes

2 cups diced cooked ham

2 cups milk

1 cup boiling water

2 cans (11 oz each) whole kernel corn with red and green peppers, drained

1 can (10¾ oz) condensed Cheddar cheese soup

1 box (7.8 oz) scalloped potatoes

1. In 3½- or 4-quart slow cooker, mix all ingredients, making sure potato slices are covered with sauce.

2. Cover; cook on Low heat setting 8 to 10 hours or until potatoes are tender.

1 Serving: Calories 610; Total Fat 18g (Saturated Fat 6g; Trans Fat 1g); Cholesterol 60mg; Sodium 3480mg; Total Carbohydrate 82g (Dietary Fiber 5g) Exchanges: 3½ Starch, 1½ Other Carbohydrate, ½ Low-Fat Milk, 2½ Lean Meat, 1 Fat Carbohydrate Choices: 5½

QuickTip

Make this into a kid's favorite by using bologna instead of the ham. You'll need about a one-pound piece of bologna for two cups diced.

prep time
15 minutes

start to finish
7 hours 15 minutes

slow cooker
3½ to 4 quart

6 servings
(1½ cups each)

Cheesy Potatoes with Ham

6 cups cubed (1-inch) peeled
    baking potatoes

1½ cups cubed cooked ham

1 can (15.25 oz) whole kernel sweet
    corn, drained

¼ cup chopped green bell pepper

2 teaspoons instant minced onion

1 can (10¾ oz) condensed Cheddar
    cheese soup

½ cup milk

2 tablespoons all-purpose flour

1. In 3½- to 4-quart slow cooker, mix potatoes, ham, corn, bell pepper and onion.

2. In small bowl, mix soup, milk and flour; beat with wire whisk until smooth. Pour soup mixture over potato mixture; stir gently to mix.

3. Cover; cook on Low heat setting 7 to 9 hours or until potatoes are tender.

1 Serving: Calories 330; Total Fat 8g (Saturated Fat 3.5g; Trans Fat 0.5g); Cholesterol 30mg; Sodium 1170mg; Total Carbohydrate 50g (Dietary Fiber 4g) **Exchanges:** 2½ Starch, 1 Other Carbohydrate, 1 Medium-Fat Meat **Carbohydrate Choices:** 3

QuickTip

If you don't have instant minced onion, use ¼ cup chopped onion instead. This cheesy potato dish is also a great way to use leftover cooked roast beef or turkey.

Bratwurst and Sauerkraut

4 cooked bratwursts (about 4 oz each), cut into ½-inch slices

2 cans (14 oz each) sauerkraut, drained

⅓ cup packed brown sugar

6 hot dog or bratwurst buns, split

1. In 3½- to 6-quart slow cooker, mix all ingredients except buns.

2. Cover; cook on Low heat setting 4 to 5 hours. Spoon bratwurst mixture into buns.

1 Sandwich: Calories 420; Total Fat 23g (Saturated Fat 8g; Trans Fat 1g); Cholesterol 45mg; Sodium 1600mg; Total Carbohydrate 40g (Dietary Fiber 4g) **Exchanges:** 1½ Starch, 1 Other Carbohydrate, 1 Vegetable, 1 High-Fat Meat, 2½ Fat **Carbohydrate Choices:** 2½

QuickTip

Be sure to use fully cooked bratwursts rather than fresh. The juice that would be released from fresh brats during cooking would add too much liquid to the mixture.

Beans 'n Hot Dogs

1 lb hot dogs, each cut into 4 pieces

3 cans (15 oz each) pork and beans
    in tomato sauce, undrained

½ cup ketchup

¼ cup finely chopped onion
    (½ medium)

¼ cup molasses

2 teaspoons yellow mustard

1. In 3½- to 4-quart slow cooker, mix all ingredients.

2. Cover; cook on Low heat setting 5 to 6 hours.

1 Serving: Calories 400; Total Fat 18g (Saturated Fat 7g; Trans Fat 0g); Cholesterol 45mg; Sodium 1570mg; Total Carbohydrate 45g (Dietary Fiber 9g) Exchanges: 2 Starch, 1 Other Carbohydrate, 1½ High-Fat Meat, 1 Fat Carbohydrate Choices: 3

QuickTip

Fully cooked bratwursts or Polish sausages can be used in place of the hot dogs in this recipe. Cut them into thick slices.

chapter four

stews, soups & chilies

Hunter's Stew with Chicken

1 medium onion, thinly sliced

1 medium green bell pepper, cut into 1-inch pieces

3 boneless skinless chicken breasts, cut into 2x1-inch pieces

1 can (15 oz) chick peas (garbanzo beans), drained

1 jar (14 oz) tomato pasta sauce

1 can (8 oz) mushroom pieces and stems, drained

1. In 3½- to 4-quart slow cooker, mix all ingredients.

2. Cover; cook on Low heat setting at least 6 hours.

1 Serving: Calories 410; Total Fat 9g (Saturated Fat 1.5g; Trans Fat 0g); Cholesterol 55mg; Sodium 910mg; Total Carbohydrate 50g (Dietary Fiber 9g) **Exchanges:** 2 Starch, 1 Other Carbohydrate, 1 Vegetable, 3 Very Lean Meat, 1 Fat **Carbohydrate Choices:** 3

Moroccan Chicken Stew

STEW

1 cup ready-to-eat baby-cut carrots

1 medium onion, chopped (½ cup)

1 tablespoon chicken bouillon
    granules

1½ teaspoons ground cumin

¼ teaspoon ground cinnamon

¼ teaspoon ground red pepper
    (cayenne)

6 boneless skinless chicken thighs
    (about 1¼ lb)

1½ cups water

3 tablespoons lemon juice

1 small zucchini (about 4 oz), cut
    into ½-inch pieces

1 small yellow summer squash
    (about 4 oz), cut into ½-inch
    pieces

1 can (15 oz) chick peas or garbanzo
    beans, drained

COUSCOUS

1 package (10 oz) uncooked
    couscous

2 cups water

1 tablespoon olive or vegetable oil

½ teaspoon salt

1. In 3½- to 4-quart slow cooker, mix carrots and onion. In small bowl, mix bouillon, cumin, cinnamon and red pepper. Sprinkle over vegetables.

2. Top vegetables with chicken thighs. Pour 1½ cups water and the lemon juice over chicken.

3. Cover; cook on Low heat setting 8 to 10 hours.

4. Gently stir zucchini, summer squash and chick peas into stew. Cover; cook 30 minutes longer. Meanwhile, during last 5 minutes of cooking, prepare couscous as directed on package, using 2 cups water, the oil and salt. Spoon couscous into individual shallow bowls. Top each with stew.

1 Serving: Calories 490; Total Fat 12g (Saturated Fat 3g; Trans Fat 0g); Cholesterol 60mg; Sodium 800mg; Total Carbohydrate 61g (Dietary Fiber 8g) **Exchanges:** 2½ Starch, 1 Other Carbohydrate, 1 Vegetable, 3½ Lean Meat Carbohydrate Choices: 4

QuickTip

You can use 1½ cups chicken broth (from a can or box) for the bouillon granules and water.

Chicken Brunswick Stew

2 tablespoons all-purpose flour

2 teaspoons chicken bouillon granules

1½ teaspoons poultry seasoning

⅛ teaspoon pepper

6 bone-in chicken thighs (about 1½ lb), skin removed

2 medium Yukon Gold potatoes (about 1 lb), cut into 1-inch pieces (about 3 cups)

½ cup chopped onion

1 can (15 oz) tomato sauce

1 tablespoon Worcestershire sauce

1 box (9 oz) frozen baby lima beans, thawed

1 box (9 oz) frozen whole kernel corn, thawed

Salt and pepper, if desired

1. In large resealable food-storage plastic bag, mix flour, bouillon, poultry seasoning and pepper. Add chicken thighs, potatoes and onion; seal bag and shake to coat. In 3½- to 4-quart slow cooker, place chicken and vegetables.

2. In small bowl, mix tomato sauce and Worcestershire sauce. Pour over chicken and vegetables; stir gently.

3. Cover; cook on Low heat setting 6 to 8 hours.

4. Stir lima beans and corn into stew. Cover; cook about 30 minutes longer or until beans and corn are tender.

5. With slotted spoon, remove chicken from slow cooker. Remove chicken from bones; discard bones. Cut chicken into pieces; return chicken to stew. Add salt and pepper to taste.

1 Serving: Calories 300; Total Fat 7g (Saturated Fat 2g; Trans Fat 0g); Cholesterol 45mg; Sodium 760mg; Total Carbohydrate 38g (Dietary Fiber 6g) **Exchanges:** 2 Starch, ½ Other Carbohydrate, 2 Lean Meat **Carbohydrate Choices:** 2½

QuickTip

Use a 10-ounce bag of frozen shelled edamame, thawed, for the lima beans. This bright green soybean is packed with nutrients.

Beef and Barley Stew

1 lb boneless beef round steak,
½ inch thick, trimmed of fat,
cut into ¾-inch pieces

2 cups frozen cut green beans

1 cup shredded carrots
(1 to 2 medium)

½ cup uncooked regular pearl
barley

1 jar (12 oz) mushroom gravy

1 jar (4.5 oz) sliced mushrooms,
drained

2½ cups water

2 teaspoons beef bouillon granules

½ teaspoon dried thyme leaves

¼ teaspoon pepper

1. In 3½- or 4-quart slow cooker, place beef, green beans, carrots, barley, gravy and mushrooms.

2. Stir together remaining ingredients. Pour over beef and vegetables; stir until mixed.

3. Cover; cook on Low heat setting 10 to 12 hours.

1 Serving: Calories 360; Total Fat 13g (Saturated Fat 4.5g; Trans Fat 0.5g); Cholesterol 75mg; Sodium 940mg; Total Carbohydrate 27g (Dietary Fiber 6g) **Exchanges:** 1 Starch, ½ Other Carbohydrate, 1 Vegetable, 4 Lean Meat **Carbohydrate Choices:** 2

Curried Beef Stew

1 cup small whole onions, peeled

1 cup ready-to-eat baby-cut carrots

12 small new potatoes, cut in half
(about 4 cups)

2 lb boneless beef chuck steak,
trimmed of fat, cut into 1½-inch
pieces

1 can (14.5 oz) diced tomatoes,
undrained

½ cup apple juice

4 teaspoons curry powder

½ teaspoon salt

¼ teaspoon pepper

1. In 3½- to 4-quart slow cooker, layer onions, carrots and potatoes. Place beef over vegetables.

2. In medium bowl, mix remaining ingredients. Pour over beef.

3. Cover; cook on Low heat setting 8 to 10 hours.

1 Serving: Calories 370; Total Fat 17g (Saturated Fat 6g; Trans Fat 0.5g); Cholesterol 80mg; Sodium 390mg; Total Carbohydrate 27g (Dietary Fiber 5g) Exchanges: 1 Starch, ½ Other Carbohydrate, 1 Vegetable, 3 Medium-Fat Meat Carbohydrate Choices: 2

QuickTip

You can use one cup frozen small whole onions (from a one-pound bag) or one small onion, cut into ½-inch pieces, for the small whole onions.

Hungarian Stew

2 lb lean boneless beef chuck roast, cut into ¾-inch pieces

2 cups ready-to-eat baby-cut carrots

1 medium onion, sliced (½ cup)

1 medium green bell pepper, sliced

⅓ cup all-purpose flour

3 teaspoons paprika

½ teaspoon salt

½ teaspoon dried thyme leaves

¼ teaspoon pepper

½ cup chili sauce

1 can (14 oz) beef broth

2 cups sliced fresh mushrooms

1 bag (16 oz) uncooked wide egg noodles (10 cups)

1 container (8 oz) sour cream

2 tablespoons chopped fresh parsley

1. In 3½- to 4-quart slow cooker, mix beef, carrots, onion and bell pepper. Add flour, paprika, salt, thyme and pepper; toss to coat. Stir in chili sauce and broth.

2. Cover; cook on Low heat setting 7 to 8 hours.

3. Stir mushrooms into stew. Cover; cook on Low heat setting 20 to 30 minutes longer or until mushrooms are tender. Meanwhile, cook noodles to desired doneness as directed on package; drain.

4. At serving time, stir sour cream into stew until well mixed. Spoon noodles into individual shallow bowls. Top each with stew. Sprinkle with parsley.

1 Serving: Calories 510; Total Fat 21g (Saturated Fat 9g; Trans Fat 1g); Cholesterol 120mg; Sodium 920mg; Total Carbohydrate 52g (Dietary Fiber 5g) **Exchanges:** 2 Starch, 1 Other Carbohydrate, 1 Vegetable, 3 Medium-Fat Meat, 1 Fat **Carbohydrate Choices:** 3½

QuickTip

A terrific time-saver is to cut up the veggies and meat for this stew the night before. Place them in separate containers, cover tightly and refrigerate until you are ready to begin.

Family-Favorite Beef Stew

1½ lb beef stew meat, cut into ¾-inch cubes

2 tablespoons all-purpose flour

1 teaspoon salt

½ teaspoon pepper

1 tablespoon vegetable oil

1 lb small red potatoes (2½ to 3 inch), quartered

1½ cups frozen small whole onions (from 1-lb bag)

1 bag (16 oz) ready-to-eat baby-cut carrots

1 jar (12 oz) beef gravy

1 can (14.5 oz) diced tomatoes, undrained

3 tablespoons all-purpose flour

¼ cup cold water

1. In large resealable food-storage plastic bag, add beef, the 2 tablespoons flour, salt and pepper; seal bag and shake to coat. In 10-inch skillet, heat oil over medium-high heat. Cook coated beef in oil 4 to 6 minutes, stirring occasionally, until browned.

2. In 4- to 6-quart slow cooker, layer potatoes, onions and carrots. Add browned beef; sprinkle with any remaining flour mixture. Top with gravy and tomatoes.

3. Cover; cook on Low heat setting 8 to 10 hours.

4. Mix 3 tablespoons flour with the cold water. Stir into stew. Increase heat setting to High. Cover; cook about 10 minutes longer or until thickened.

1 Serving: Calories 390; Total Fat 16g (Saturated Fat 6g; Trans Fat 0.5g); Cholesterol 60mg; Sodium 920mg; Total Carbohydrate 36g (Dietary Fiber 5g) **Exchanges:** 1 Starch, ½ Other Carbohydrate, 2 Vegetable, 2½ Lean Meat, 2 Fat **Carbohydrate Choices:** 2½

Meatball-Bean Stew

1 medium onion, coarsely chopped (½ cup)

1 can (16 oz) baked beans, undrained

1 can (14.5 oz) stewed tomatoes with Italian herbs, undrained

1 box (12 oz) frozen cooked Italian-style meatballs

1 medium zucchini, halved lengthwise, sliced (2 cups)

1 cup frozen mixed vegetables, thawed

1. In 3½- to 4-quart slow cooker, mix onion, baked beans, tomatoes and meatballs.

2. Cover; cook on Low heat setting 6 to 7 hours.

3. Stir in zucchini and mixed vegetables. Increase heat setting to High. Cover; cook 20 to 30 minutes longer or until vegetables are tender.

1 Serving: Calories 410; Total Fat 13g (Saturated Fat 5g; Trans Fat 0.5g); Cholesterol 95mg; Sodium 1290mg; Total Carbohydrate 48g (Dietary Fiber 10g) Exchanges: 1 Starch, 1½ Other Carbohydrate, 1½ Vegetable, 3 Lean Meat, 1 Fat Carbohydrate Choices: 3

Italian Meatball Stew

1 bag (16 oz) frozen cooked Italian-style meatballs, thawed

1 cup frozen small whole onions

½ teaspoon salt

2 cans (14.5 oz each) diced tomatoes with Italian-style herbs, undrained

2 tablespoons all-purpose flour

2 tablespoons water

2½ cups frozen bell pepper and onion stir-fry, thawed, drained

¼ cup shredded fresh Parmesan cheese (1 oz)

1. In 3½- to 4-quart slow cooker, mix meatballs, onions, salt and tomatoes.

2. Cover; cook on Low heat setting 6 to 8 hours.

3. In small bowl, blend flour and water until smooth. Stir flour mixture into stew. Stir in bell pepper and onion stir-fry. Increase heat setting to High. Cover; cook 15 to 20 minutes longer or until stew has thickened and bell peppers are hot. Sprinkle individual servings with cheese.

1 Serving: Calories 430; Total Fat 18g (Saturated Fat 7g; Trans Fat 1g); Cholesterol 125mg; Sodium 1350mg; Total Carbohydrate 37g (Dietary Fiber 5g) **Exchanges:** 1 Starch, 1 Other Carbohydrate, 2 Vegetable, 3 Medium-Fat Meat **Carbohydrate Choices:** 2½

Home-Style Pork Stew

1 tablespoon vegetable oil

1½ lb boneless pork shoulder roast, cut into 1½-inch pieces

⅛ teaspoon salt

⅛ teaspoon pepper

8 small unpeeled red potatoes, quartered (4 cups)

2 cups ready-to-eat baby-cut carrots, cut in half lengthwise

1 jar (12 oz) pork gravy

2 tablespoons ketchup

½ teaspoon dried rosemary leaves

¼ teaspoon pepper

⅛ teaspoon ground sage

1½ cups frozen cut green beans, thawed

1. In 10-inch skillet, heat oil over high heat until hot. Add pork; sprinkle with salt and ⅛ teaspoon pepper. Cook 3 to 5 minutes, stirring frequently, until browned.

2. In 3½- to 4-quart slow cooker, mix pork and remaining ingredients except green beans.

3. Cover; cook on Low heat setting 7 to 8 hours.

4. Stir thawed green beans into stew. Increase heat setting to High. Cover; cook 15 to 20 minutes longer or until green beans are tender.

1 Serving: Calories 380; Total Fat 17g (Saturated Fat 6g; Trans Fat 0g); Cholesterol 75mg; Sodium 500mg; Total Carbohydrate 28g (Dietary Fiber 4g) Exchanges: 1 Starch, ½ Other Carbohydrate, 1 Vegetable, 3½ Lean Meat, 1 Fat Carbohydrate Choices: 2

QuickTip

In a rush? Skip the pork-browning step. The recipe may have a bit less color, but saving prep and cleanup time on busy days is worth it.

Smoky Ham and Navy Bean Stew

1 lb cooked ham, cut into ½-inch cubes (3 cups)

2 cups water

1 cup dried navy beans

2 medium stalks celery, sliced (1 cup)

2 medium carrots, sliced (1 cup)

1 small onion, chopped (¼ cup)

¼ teaspoon dried thyme leaves

¼ teaspoon liquid smoke

¼ cup chopped fresh parsley

1. In 3½- to 4-quart slow cooker, mix all ingredients except parsley.

2. Cover; cook on Low heat setting 10 to 12 hours.

3. Just before serving, stir in parsley.

1 Serving: Calories 390; Total Fat 11g (Saturated Fat 3.5g; Trans Fat 0g); Cholesterol 65mg; Sodium 1740mg; Total Carbohydrate 36g (Dietary Fiber 14g) Exchanges: 2 Starch, 1 Vegetable, 4 Very Lean Meat, 1½ Fat Carbohydrate Choices: 2½

QuickTip

Liquid smoke is exactly that—liquid mixed with smoke. It lends a smoky, hickory flavor to this bean stew. Look for it in the condiment aisle of the grocery store. If you like, you can omit it and the stew will still be tasty.

prep time
15 minutes

start to finish
6 hours 25 minutes

slow cooker
3½ to 4 quart

8 servings
(1⅓ cups each)

Italian Ravioli Stew

4 medium carrots, sliced (2 cups)

1 large onion, chopped (1 cup)

2 cans (14.5 oz each) diced tomatoes with Italian-style herbs, undrained

2 cans (14 oz each) chicken broth

1 can (19 oz) cannellini beans, drained

2 teaspoons dried basil leaves

1 package (9 oz) refrigerated Italian sausage- or cheese-filled ravioli

1. In 3½- to 4-quart slow cooker, mix all ingredients except ravioli. Cover; cook on Low heat setting about 6 hours or until vegetables are tender.

2. Increase heat setting to High. Stir in ravioli. Cover; cook about 8 minutes longer or until ravioli are tender.

1 Serving: Calories 240; Total Fat 4.5g (Saturated Fat 2.5g; Trans Fat 0g); Cholesterol 15mg; Sodium 880mg; Total Carbohydrate 37g (Dietary Fiber 6g) **Exchanges:** 1½ Starch, ½ Other Carbohydrate, 1½ Vegetable, ½ High-Fat Meat **Carbohydrate Choices:** 2½

QuickTip

Try other flavors of ravioli such as chicken and prosciutto or garlic and mozzarella.

Lentil and Pasta Stew

¾ cup dried lentils, sorted, rinsed

2 medium stalks celery, sliced (1 cup)

½ cup coarsely chopped green bell pepper

3½ cups vegetable broth

1 can (11.5 oz) vegetable juice

⅓ cup uncooked rosamarina or orzo pasta (2 oz)

1 teaspoon dried thyme leaves

1. In 3½- to 4-quart slow cooker, mix lentils, celery, bell pepper and broth.

2. Cover; cook on Low heat setting 10 to 12 hours.

3. Stir vegetable juice, pasta and thyme into stew. Increase heat setting to High. Cover; cook 25 to 30 minutes longer or until pasta is tender.

1 Serving: Calories 220; Total Fat 1g (Saturated Fat 0g; Trans Fat 0g); Cholesterol 0mg; Sodium 1110mg; Total Carbohydrate 40g (Dietary Fiber 8g) **Exchanges:** 1½ Starch, 1 Other Carbohydrate, 1 Very Lean Meat **Carbohydrate Choices:** 2½

QuickTip

Lentils come in many colors—brown, red and yellow. You can find brown lentils in most supermarkets, but you may have to look in a specialty market to find the red and yellow varieties.

Ratatouille Bean Stew

1 cup dried chick peas or garbanzo beans, sorted, rinsed

1 medium onion, chopped (½ cup)

2 cloves garlic, finely chopped

1 can (14 oz) chicken broth

1 jar (4.5 oz) sliced mushrooms, drained

¼ teaspoon salt

1 large zucchini, sliced

1 medium red or green bell pepper, cut into pieces

1 teaspoon Italian seasoning

1 can (14.5 oz) diced tomatoes with Italian-style herbs, undrained

1. Soak chick peas in enough water to cover for at least 8 hours. Drain, discarding water.

2. In 3½- to 4-quart slow cooker, mix chick peas, onion, garlic, broth, mushrooms and salt.

3. Cover; cook on Low heat setting 10 to 12 hours.

4. Stir zucchini, bell pepper, Italian seasoning and tomatoes into stew. Increase heat setting to High. Cover; cook 30 to 35 minutes longer or until vegetables are tender.

1 Serving: Calories 210; Total Fat 3g (Saturated Fat 0g; Trans Fat 0g); Cholesterol 0mg; Sodium 700mg; Total Carbohydrate 34g (Dietary Fiber 9g) Exchanges: 1 Starch, ½ Other Carbohydrate, 2 Vegetable, ½ Very Lean Meat, ½ Fat Carbohydrate Choices: 2

Chicken Tortilla Soup

**6 boneless skinless chicken thighs
(1¼ lb)**

**1½ cups frozen whole kernel corn,
thawed**

¾ cup salsa verde

1 teaspoon dried oregano leaves

**1 can (15 oz) chick peas or garbanzo
beans, drained, rinsed**

1 can (4.5 oz) chopped green chiles

2 cans (14 oz each) chicken broth

2 tomatoes, seeded, chopped

Chopped fresh cilantro, if desired

1. In 3- to 4-quart slow cooker, mix all ingredients except tomatoes and cilantro.

2. Cover; cook on Low heat setting 5 to 7.

3. Stir to break up chicken thighs. Stir in tomatoes before serving. Garnish with cilantro.

1 Serving: Calories 330; Total Fat 9g (Saturated Fat 2.5g; Trans Fat 0g); Cholesterol 45mg; Sodium 1160mg; Total Carbohydrate 37g (Dietary Fiber 7g) **Exchanges:** 1½ Starch, ½ Other Carbohydrate, 1 Vegetable, 3 Lean Meat Carbohydrate Choices: 2½

QuickTip

Salsa verde is "green salsa," which is made from tomatillos, green chiles and cilantro. You can use ¾ cup tomato salsa if you don't have salsa verde.

Chicken-Vegetable Chowder

1 lb boneless skinless chicken
    thighs, cut into 1-inch pieces

1 cup ready-to-eat baby-cut carrots,
    cut in half lengthwise

1 cup sliced fresh mushrooms

1 medium onion, chopped (½ cup)

½ cup water

¼ teaspoon garlic powder

⅛ teaspoon dried thyme leaves

1 can (14 oz) chicken broth

1 can (10¾ oz) condensed
    98%-fat-free cream of chicken
    soup with 30% less sodium

½ cup milk

3 tablespoons all-purpose flour

1 box (9 oz) frozen cut broccoli
    (2 cups), thawed

1. In 3- to 4-quart slow cooker, mix chicken, carrots, mushrooms, onion, water, garlic powder, thyme and broth.

2. Cover; cook on Low heat setting 7 to 9 hours.

3. Skim fat from slow cooker. In small bowl, beat soup, milk and flour with wire whisk until smooth. Add soup mixture and broccoli to chicken mixture. Cover; cook about 30 minutes longer or until broccoli is tender.

1 Serving: Calories 260; Total Fat 10g (Saturated Fat 3g; Trans Fat 0g); Cholesterol 60mg; Sodium 660mg; Total Carbohydrate 17g (Dietary Fiber 3g) **Exchanges:** ½ Starch, ½ Other Carbohydrate, 1 Vegetable, 3 Lean Meat **Carbohydrate Choices:** 1

Dill-Turkey Chowder

1 lb uncooked turkey breast slices,
   cut into 1-inch pieces

¾ teaspoon garlic-pepper blend

½ teaspoon salt

6 to 8 small red potatoes, cut into
   1-inch pieces

1 medium onion, chopped (½ cup)

2 medium carrots, sliced (1 cup)

2 teaspoons dried dill weed

2½ cups chicken broth

1 can (15.25 oz) whole kernel corn,
   drained

1 cup half-and-half

3 tablespoons cornstarch

1. In 4- to 5-quart slow cooker, place turkey; sprinkle with garlic-pepper blend and salt. Add remaining ingredients except half-and-half and cornstarch; mix well.

2. Cover; cook on Low heat setting 6 to 8 hours.

3. In small bowl, mix half-and-half and cornstarch until smooth. Gradually stir into chowder. Increase heat setting to High. Cover; cook about 20 minutes longer, stirring occasionally, until thickened.

1 Serving: Calories 370; Total Fat 7g (Saturated Fat 3.5g; Trans Fat 0g); Cholesterol 65mg; Sodium 900mg; Total Carbohydrate 51g (Dietary Fiber 6g) **Exchanges:** 2½ Starch, 1 Other Carbohydrate, 2½ Very Lean Meat, ½ Fat **Carbohydrate Choices:** 3½

QuickTip

A pound of boneless skinless chicken thighs, cut into one-inch pieces, can be used for the turkey breast.

Hamburger and Noodle Soup

1 lb lean (at least 80%) ground beef

1 medium onion, coarsely chopped (½ cup)

1 stalk celery, cut into ¼-inch slices

1 package (1.15 oz) beefy mushroom soup and recipe mix

1 can (14.5 oz) diced tomatoes, undrained

3 cups water

½ teaspoon salt

¼ teaspoon pepper

2 cups frozen mixed vegetables, thawed

1 cup uncooked fine egg noodles (2 oz)

1. In 10-inch skillet, cook beef over medium-high heat 5 to 7 minutes, stirring frequently, until thoroughly cooked; drain.

2. In 4- to 6-quart slow cooker, mix beef and all remaining ingredients except mixed vegetables and noodles.

3. Cover; cook on Low heat setting 6 to 8 hours.

4. Stir in thawed vegetables and egg noodles. Increase heat setting to High. Cover; cook 15 to 20 minutes longer or until vegetables are crisp-tender and noodles are tender.

1 Serving: Calories 240; Total Fat 9g (Saturated Fat 3.5g; Trans Fat 0.5g); Cholesterol 55mg; Sodium 450mg; Total Carbohydrate 23g (Dietary Fiber 4g) **Exchanges:** 1 Other Carbohydrate, 2 Vegetable, 2 Medium-Fat Meat **Carbohydrate Choices:** 1½

QuickTip

Be sure to set the slow cooker on High so vegetables and noodles cook faster. Add these ingredients quickly and replace the slow cooker's lid right away to minimize heat loss.

Vegetable Beef Soup

1 lb beef stew meat, cut into bite-sized pieces if needed

½ lb small red potatoes, each cut into 8 pieces (about 1½ cups)

1 medium onion, chopped (½ cup)

4 cloves garlic, finely chopped

1 teaspoon seasoned salt

½ teaspoon pepper

2 bay leaves

2 cans (14 oz each) beef broth

1 can (14 oz) diced tomatoes, undrained

1 can (15 to 16 oz) great northern beans, drained, rinsed

2 cups frozen mixed vegetables, thawed

1. In 3- to 4-quart slow cooker, mix all ingredients except frozen vegetables.

2. Cover; cook on Low heat setting 7 to 8 hours.

3. Add mixed vegetables. Increase heat setting to High. Cover; cook 20 to 30 minutes longer or until vegetables are crisp-tender. Remove bay leaves before serving.

1 Serving: Calories 330; Total Fat 10g (Saturated Fat 3.5g; Trans Fat 0g); Cholesterol 45mg; Sodium 950mg; Total Carbohydrate 35g (Dietary Fiber 8g) **Exchanges:** 1½ Starch, ½ Other Carbohydrate, 1 Vegetable, 2½ Lean Meat, ½ Fat **Carbohydrate Choices:** 2

QuickTip

Let the frozen veggies thaw in the refrigerator while the soup is cooking in the slow cooker.

Wild Rice and Mushroom Soup

1 lb small whole mushrooms, halved

½ cup uncooked whole-grain wild rice (not cracked or broken)

1 medium stalk celery, cut into ½-inch pieces (½ cup)

2 medium carrots, cut into ½-inch pieces (1 cup)

1 package (0.9 oz) onion mushroom soup mix (from 1.8-oz box)

1 tablespoon sugar

1 cup water

1 carton (32 oz) beef broth

1 cup frozen sweet peas, thawed

1. In 3- to 4-quart slow cooker, layer mushrooms, rice, celery, carrots, soup mix and sugar. Pour water and broth over top.

2. Cover; cook on Low heat setting 6 to 8 hours.

3. Gently stir thawed peas into soup. Cover; cook about 10 minutes longer or until peas are hot.

1 Serving: Calories 130; Total Fat 1g (Saturated Fat 0g; Trans Fat 0g); Cholesterol 0mg; Sodium 1060mg; Total Carbohydrate 24g (Dietary Fiber 3g) **Exchanges:** 1 Starch, ½ Other Carbohydrate, 1 Vegetable **Carbohydrate Choices:** 1½

QuickTip

Use whole-grain wild rice for this soup; rice labeled broken or cracked loses its shape during long slow cooking.

Italian Sausage–Vegetable Soup

½ lb bulk Italian pork sausage

2 medium carrots, sliced (1 cup)

1 large baking potato, peeled, cut into ½-inch cubes

1 clove garlic, finely chopped

2 cans (14 oz each) beef broth

1 can (15 oz) chick peas (garbanzo beans), drained

1 can (14.5 oz) chunky diced tomatoes (pasta style), undrained

1½ cups water

½ teaspoon Italian seasoning

1 bay leaf

1 cup julienne (matchstick-cut) zucchini

¼ cup shredded Parmesan cheese (1 oz), if desired

1. In 10-inch skillet, cook sausage over medium-high heat, stirring frequently, until thoroughly cooked; drain. In 3½- to 4-quart slow cooker, stir cooked sausage and remaining ingredients except zucchini and cheese until mixed.

2. Cover; cook on Low heat setting 7 to 9 hours.

3. Discard bay leaf. Gently stir in zucchini. Cover; cook about 30 minutes longer or until zucchini is tender.

4. To serve, ladle soup into individual bowls. Sprinkle with cheese.

1 Serving: Calories 210; Total Fat 6g (Saturated Fat 1.5g; Trans Fat 0g); Cholesterol 15mg; Sodium 780mg; Total Carbohydrate 28g (Dietary Fiber 5g) **Exchanges:** 1½ Starch, 1 Vegetable, ½ Very Lean Meat, 1 Fat **Carbohydrate Choices:** 2

Confetti Yellow Pea Soup

1 bag (16 oz) dried yellow split peas, rinsed

4 cups water

1 can (10½ oz) condensed chicken broth

1 cup julienne (matchstick-cut) carrots

6 oz chorizo sausage, casing removed, cut into ¼-inch slices

¼ teaspoon salt

¼ teaspoon pepper

8 medium green onions, sliced (½ cup)

1 can (11 oz) whole kernel corn with red and green peppers

1. In 3½- to 4-quart slow cooker, gently mix all ingredients except onions and corn.

2. Cover; cook on Low heat setting 7 to 9 hours or until peas are soft.

3. Stir in onions and corn. Cover; cook about 30 minutes longer or until corn is hot.

1 Serving: Calories 420; Total Fat 12g (Saturated Fat 4.5g; Trans Fat 0g); Cholesterol 25mg; Sodium 780mg; Total Carbohydrate 51g (Dietary Fiber 22g) **Exchanges:** 2½ Starch, ½ Other Carbohydrate, 1 Vegetable, 2 Lean Meat, 1 Fat **Carbohydrate Choices:** 3½

Split Pea Soup with Veggies

1 ham bone, 2 lb ham shanks or 2 lb smoked pork hocks

1 bag (16 oz) dried split peas (2 cups), sorted, rinsed

1 large onion, chopped (1 cup)

2 medium stalks celery, finely chopped (1 cup)

¼ teaspoon pepper

7 cups water

3 medium carrots, cut into ¼-inch slices (1½ cups)

1. In 4- to 6-quart slow cooker, gently mix all ingredients except carrots.

2. Cover; cook on Low heat setting 3 to 4 hours.

3. Remove ham bone from soup. Let stand about 15 minutes or until cool enough to handle.

4. Remove ham from bone. Remove excess fat from ham; cut ham into ½-inch pieces. Stir ham and carrots into soup. Increase heat setting to High. Cover; cook about 15 minutes longer or until carrots are tender.

1 Serving: Calories 240; Total Fat 3g (Saturated Fat 1g; Trans Fat 0g); Cholesterol 20mg; Sodium 45mg; Total Carbohydrate 34g (Dietary Fiber 16g) **Exchanges:** 2 Starch, 1 Vegetable, 1½ Very Lean Meat **Carbohydrate Choices:** 2

QuickTip

To sort the split peas, remove any grit or discolored peas. Place the split peas in a bowl, and cover them with water. After a minute or two, remove any skins or split peas that float to the top. Finally, rinse the split peas in a colander or strainer.

Fish and Rice Chowder

2 medium stalks celery, chopped (1 cup)

1 medium green bell pepper, chopped

1 medium onion, chopped (½ cup)

2 cloves garlic, finely chopped

2 cans (14.5 oz each) diced tomatoes, undrained

2 cups vegetable juice

1 cup dry white wine or vegetable broth

1 tablespoon Worcestershire sauce

1 teaspoon salt

¼ teaspoon ground red pepper (cayenne)

1 lb firm-fleshed fish steak (halibut, haddock, tuna or red snapper), cut into 1-inch pieces

½ cup uncooked instant white rice

3 tablespoons chopped fresh parsley

1. In 3½- to 6-quart slow cooker, mix celery, bell pepper, onion, garlic, tomatoes, vegetable juice, wine, Worcestershire sauce, salt and red pepper.

2. Cover; cook on Low heat setting 7 to 9 hours or on High heat setting 3 to 4 hours.

3. Stir fish, rice and parsley into chowder. Increase heat setting to High. Cover; cook 30 to 45 minutes longer or until fish flakes easily with fork.

1 Serving: Calories 200; Total Fat 1.5g (Saturated Fat 0g; Trans Fat 0g); Cholesterol 40mg; Sodium 910mg; Total Carbohydrate 27g (Dietary Fiber 3g) **Exchanges:** 1 Starch, ½ Other Carbohydrate, 1½ Vegetable, 1½ Very Lean Meat **Carbohydrate Choices:** 2

QuickTip

You can use ¼ teaspoon garlic powder or ½ teaspoon instant minced garlic if you don't have fresh garlic on hand.

prep time
15 minutes

start to finish
8 hours 20 minutes

slow cooker
3½ to 4 quart

8 servings
(1½ cups each)

Curried Lentil Soup

1 bag (16 oz) dried lentils, sorted, rinsed (2½ cups)

8 cups water

2 medium carrots, cut into ½-inch slices (1 cup)

2 medium stalks celery, cut into ½-inch slices (1 cup)

1 medium onion, chopped (½ cup)

2 cloves garlic, finely chopped

2 extra-large vegetarian vegetable bouillon cubes or 2 chicken bouillon cubes

3 teaspoons curry powder

1 teaspoon salt

2 bay leaves

1 can (14.5 oz) diced tomatoes, undrained

2 cups baby or coarsely chopped fresh spinach

½ cup plain low-fat yogurt

1. In 3½- or 4-quart slow cooker, mix all ingredients except tomatoes, spinach and yogurt.

2. Cover; cook on Low heat setting 8 to 9 hours.

3. Stir in tomatoes. Cover; cook about 5 minutes longer or until hot.

4. Just before serving, discard bay leaves. Top individual servings with ¼ cup spinach and 1 tablespoon yogurt.

1 Serving: Calories 230; Total Fat 1g (Saturated Fat 0g; Trans Fat 0g); Cholesterol 0mg; Sodium 700mg; Total Carbohydrate 39g (Dietary Fiber 11g) **Exchanges:** 2 Starch, 1 Vegetable, 1 Very Lean Meat **Carbohydrate Choices:** 2½

QuickTip

Acidic ingredients, such as tomatoes, prevent lentils from cooking until they are tender. Add the tomatoes after the lentils have cooked completely and are tender.

Two-Bean Minestrone

2 medium carrots, cut into ½-inch slices (1 cup)

1 medium onion, halved crosswise, cut into thin wedges

1 clove garlic, finely chopped

1 stalk celery, coarsely chopped (⅓ cup)

2 cans (14 oz each) chicken broth

1 can (19 oz) white kidney or cannellini beans, drained, rinsed

1 can (15.5 or 15 oz) kidney beans, drained, rinsed

1 can (14.5 oz) Italian-style stewed tomatoes, undrained, cut up

½ teaspoon salt

⅛ teaspoon pepper

1 cup frozen cut leaf spinach, thawed, squeezed to drain (from 1 lb bag)

3 oz uncooked spaghetti, broken into thirds (¾ cup)

1. In 3½- to 4-quart slow cooker, mix all ingredients except spinach and spaghetti.

2. Cover; cook on Low heat setting 7 to 10 hours or until vegetables are tender.

3. Stir in thawed spinach and spaghetti. Increase heat setting to High. Cover; cook 15 to 20 minutes longer or until spaghetti is tender.

1 Serving: Calories 310; Total Fat 2g (Saturated Fat 0g; Trans Fat 0g); Cholesterol 0mg; Sodium 900mg; Total Carbohydrate 53g (Dietary Fiber 12g) **Exchanges:** 2 Starch, 1 Other Carbohydrate, 1 Vegetable, 1½ Very Lean Meat **Carbohydrate Choices:** 3½

QuickTip

To quickly thaw spinach, place in colander or strainer; rinse with warm water until thawed. Squeeze dry with paper towels.

prep time
5 minutes

start to finish
8 hours 20 minutes

slow cooker
3 to 4 quart

6 servings
(1⅓ cups each)

Italian Bean and Pasta Soup

2 cans (19 oz each) cannellini beans, drained

1 bag (1 lb) frozen mixed vegetables

1 can (14.5 oz) diced tomatoes with basil, garlic and oregano, undrained

½ teaspoon salt

1 can (11.5 oz) vegetable juice

1 cup water

½ cup uncooked penne or mostaccioli pasta (1½ oz)

¼ cup pesto

1. In 3- to 4-quart slow cooker, mix all ingredients except pasta and pesto.

2. Cover; cook on Low heat setting 8 to 9 hours.

3. Stir penne into soup. Increase heat setting to High. Cover; cook 15 to 20 minutes longer or until penne is tender.

4. To serve, top individual servings with 2 teaspoons pesto.

1 Serving: Calories 370; Total Fat 6g (Saturated Fat 1.5g; Trans Fat 0g); Cholesterol 0mg; Sodium 1020mg; Total Carbohydrate 59g (Dietary Fiber 14g) Exchanges: 2 Starch, 1 Other Carbohydrate, 2 Vegetable, 1½ Very Lean Meat, 1 Fat Carbohydrate Choices: 4

...with Chicken

1. In 3½- to 4-quart slow cooker, mix chicken, beans, onion, garlic, oregano, salt, soup and water.

2. Cover; cook on Low heat setting 9 to 10 hours.

3. Just before serving, stir cumin, pepper sauce and chiles into chili. If desired, serve with additional pepper sauce. Serve with sour cream and chopped avocado.

1 medium onion, chopped (½ cup)

1 clove garlic, finely chopped

2 teaspoons dried oregano leaves

½ teaspoon salt

1 can (10¾ oz) condensed cream of chicken soup

5 cups water

1 teaspoon ground cumin

¼ teaspoon red pepper sauce

1 can (4.5 oz) chopped green chiles

Sour cream, if desired

Chopped avocado, if desired

1 Serving: Calories 290; Total Fat 10g (Saturated Fat 3g; Trans Fat 0g); Cholesterol 50mg; Sodium 700mg; Total Carbohydrate 27g (Dietary Fiber 6g) **Exchanges:** 2 Starch, 2½ Lean Meat **Carbohydrate Choices:** 2

Spicy Southwest Beef and Bean Chili

1½ lb boneless beef round steak, ½ inch thick, cut into ¾-inch pieces

1 medium onion, chopped (½ cup)

4 cans (8 oz each) no-salt-added tomato sauce

1 can (15.25 oz) whole kernel sweet corn, drained

1 can (15 oz) black beans, drained, rinsed

1 can (4.5 oz) chopped green chiles

2 tablespoons chili powder

1. In 4- to 5-quart slow cooker, mix all ingredients.

2. Cover; cook on Low heat setting 8 to 9 hours.

1 Serving: Calories 400; Total Fat 6g (Saturated Fat 2g; Trans Fat 0g); Cholesterol 85mg; Sodium 370mg; Total Carbohydrate 44g (Dietary Fiber 11g) **Exchanges:** 2 Starch, ½ Other Carbohydrate, 1 Vegetable, 5 Very Lean Meat **Carbohydrate Choices:** 3

QuickTip

You can use other kinds of canned beans, such as kidney, pinto or great northern, for the black beans.

Six-Can Chili

½ cup barbecue sauce

¼ cup cornmeal

1 teaspoon paprika

2 cans (15 oz each) chili without beans

1 can (28 oz) tomatoes (3 cups), undrained, cut up

1 can (15.5 oz) pinto beans or kidney beans, undrained

1 can (15 oz) caliente-style chili beans, undrained

1 can (10 oz) condensed French onion soup

Shredded Cheddar cheese, if desired

Sour cream, if desired

1. In 3½- to 4-quart slow cooker, mix all ingredients except cheese and sour cream.

2. Cover; cook on High heat setting 2 to 4 hours to allow flavors to blend. Serve with Cheddar cheese and sour cream.

1 Serving: Calories 310; Total Fat 6g (Saturated Fat 2g; Trans Fat 0g); Cholesterol 15mg; Sodium 1490mg; Total Carbohydrate 48g (Dietary Fiber 10g) Exchanges: 2 Starch, 1 Other Carbohydrate, 1½ Lean Meat Carbohydrate Choices: 3

QuickTip

If you would like to start the chili in the morning for dinner, cook it on Low heat setting eight to nine hours.

chapter five

hearty warm sandwiches

Teriyaki Barbecued Chicken Sandwiches

2½ lb boneless skinless chicken thighs

½ cup ketchup

¼ cup stir-fry sauce

1 package (1 oz) stir-fry seasoning mix

2½ cups coleslaw mix (from 16-oz bag)

10 kaiser rolls, split

1. In 3½- to 4-quart slow cooker, place chicken. In small bowl, mix ketchup, stir-fry sauce and stir-fry seasoning mix. Pour over chicken.

2. Cover; cook on Low heat setting 6 to 7 hours.

3. Remove chicken from slow cooker; place on cutting board. With 2 forks, pull chicken into shreds. Return chicken to slow cooker; stir to mix with sauce.

4. To serve, place ¼ cup coleslaw on bottom half of each roll. With slotted spoon, top each with chicken. Cover each with top half of roll.

1 Sandwich: Calories 360; Total Fat 11g (Saturated Fat 3g; Trans Fat 0.5g); Cholesterol 70mg; Sodium 900mg; Total Carbohydrate 34g (Dietary Fiber 1g) Exchanges: 1½ Starch, 1 Other Carbohydrate, 3½ Lean Meat Carbohydrate Choices: 2

QuickTip

Toting the sandwich filling to a gathering? Loop a large, sturdy rubber band from handle to handle across the slow cooker cover to keep the cooker sealed during transit.

prep time
15 minutes

start to finish
7 hours 15 minutes

slow cooker
3½ to 4 quart

12 servings
(2 tacos each)

Chicken-Bean Tacos

1¼ lb boneless skinless chicken thighs

3 tablespoons taco seasoning mix (from 1.25-oz package)

1 can (4.5 oz) chopped green chiles

1 can (8 oz) tomato sauce

1 teaspoon ground cumin

1 teaspoon coriander seed, crushed

1 can (19 oz) cannellini beans, drained

2 boxes (4.6 oz each) taco shells (24 shells total)

1½ cups shredded Cheddar cheese (6 oz)

1½ cups shredded lettuce

1 container (8 oz) sour cream

1 cup chunky-style salsa

1. In 3½- or 4-quart slow cooker, place chicken thighs. Sprinkle with taco seasoning mix. Top with chiles. In medium bowl, mix tomato sauce, cumin and coriander seed. Pour over top. Top with beans.

2. Cover; cook on Low heat setting 7 to 8 hours.

3. Remove chicken from slow cooker; place on cutting board. Mash beans in slow cooker. Shred chicken with 2 forks; return to slow cooker, and mix well.

4. To serve, spoon about 3 tablespoons chicken mixture into each taco shell. Top each with 1 tablespoon cheese, 1 tablespoon lettuce, 2 teaspoons sour cream and 2 teaspoons salsa.

1 Serving: Calories 350; Total Fat 17g (Saturated Fat 8g; Trans Fat 2g); Cholesterol 55mg; Sodium 710mg; Total Carbohydrate 29g (Dietary Fiber 4g) **Exchanges:** 1½ Starch, ½ Other Carbohydrate, 2 Lean Meat, 2 Fat **Carbohydrate Choices:** 2

prep time
15 minutes

start to finish
6 hours 15 minutes

slow cooker
4 to 6 quart

4 sandwiches

Greek Chicken Pita Folds

1 medium onion, halved, sliced

1 clove garlic, finely chopped

1 lb boneless skinless chicken thighs

1½ teaspoons lemon-pepper seasoning

½ teaspoon dried oregano leaves

¼ teaspoon ground allspice

4 pita (pocket) breads

½ cup plain yogurt

1 plum (Roma) tomato, sliced

½ medium cucumber, chopped (about ½ cup)

1. In 4- to 6-quart slow cooker, mix onion, garlic, chicken thighs, lemon-pepper seasoning, oregano and allspice; mix to coat chicken with seasoning.

2. Cover; cook on Low heat setting 6 to 8 hours.

3. Heat pita breads as directed on package. Meanwhile, remove chicken from slow cooker; place on cutting board. Shred chicken with 2 forks.

4. To serve, stir yogurt into onion mixture in slow cooker. Spoon chicken onto warm pita breads. With slotted spoon, transfer onion mixture onto chicken; top with tomato and cucumber. Fold each pita bread in half.

1 Sandwich: Calories 340; Total Fat 10g (Saturated Fat 3g; Trans Fat 0g); Cholesterol 75mg; Sodium 460mg; . Total Carbohydrate 32g (Dietary Fiber 2g) Exchanges: 1 Starch, 1 Other Carbohydrate, 4 Very Lean Meat, 1½ Fat Carbohydrate Choices: 2

QuickTip

If you don't have lemon-pepper seasoning, substitute ¾ teaspoon salt, ¼ teaspoon pepper and one teaspoon grated lemon peel.

Jerked Chicken Hoagies

3 tablespoons Caribbean jerk seasoning (dry)

3 lb boneless skinless chicken thighs

1 large red or green bell pepper, chopped (1½ cups)

1 large onion, chopped (1 cup)

½ cup chicken broth

¼ cup ketchup

6 hoagie buns, split

1. Rub jerk seasoning generously over chicken thighs. In 3½- to 4-quart slow cooker, mix bell pepper and onion. Place chicken over vegetables.

2. In small bowl, mix broth and ketchup. Pour broth mixture over chicken.

3. Cover; cook on Low heat setting 6 to 8 hours.

4. Remove chicken from slow cooker; place on cutting board. Shred chicken with 2 forks; return to slow cooker and mix well.

5. To serve, with slotted spoon, spoon chicken mixture into buns.

1 Sandwich: Calories 650; Total Fat 22g (Saturated Fat 7g; Trans Fat 1g); Cholesterol 140mg; Sodium 1190mg; Total Carbohydrate 53g (Dietary Fiber 3g) **Exchanges:** 2½ Starch, 1 Other Carbohydrate, 7 Lean Meat **Carbohydrate Choices:** 3½

QuickTip

Caribbean jerk seasoning, also known as Jamaican jerk seasoning, is generally a combination of peppers, thyme and allspice. Some blends may also contain cinnamon, ginger, cloves, garlic and onions.

prep time
15 minutes

start to finish
7 hours 15 minutes

slow cooker
3½ to 4 quart

12 sandwiches

Hot Turkey Sandwiches

2 boneless whole turkey breast
  halves (2 to 2½ lb each)
½ teaspoon salt
½ teaspoon pepper
1 can (10¾ oz) condensed cream
  of chicken soup
12 wheat or white burger buns, split
Cranberry sauce, if desired

1. Spray 3½- to 4-quart slow cooker with cooking spray. In slow cooker, place turkey breast halves. Sprinkle with salt and pepper.

2. Cover; cook on Low heat setting 7 to 8 hours.

3. Remove turkey from slow cooker; cool slightly. Remove ⅔ cup juices from slow cooker; place in 1-quart saucepan. Add soup; mix well. Cook over medium heat about 5 minutes, stirring occasionally, until hot.

4. To serve, cut turkey into slices; place on bottom halves of buns. Pour gravy over turkey. Cover with top halves of buns. Serve sandwiches with cranberry sauce.

1 Sandwich. Calories 260; Total Fat 4.5g (Saturated Fat 1g; Trans Fat 0g); Cholesterol 80mg; Sodium 480mg; Total Carbohydrate 23g (Dietary Fiber 1g) **Exchanges:** 1½ Starch, 4 Very Lean Meat **Carbohydrate Choices:** 1½

QuickTip

Don't have a can of cream of chicken soup on the shelf? Use any cream soup you have on hand such as cream of mushroom or cream of celery.

prep time
15 minutes

start to finish
8 hours 15 minutes

slow cooker
4 to 6 quart

12 sandwiches

Georgia-Style Barbecued Turkey Sandwiches

4 turkey thighs (about 3 lb), skin removed

½ cup packed brown sugar

¼ cup yellow mustard

2 tablespoons ketchup

2 tablespoons cider vinegar

2 tablespoons Louisiana-style hot pepper sauce

1 teaspoon salt

1 teaspoon coarse ground black pepper

1 teaspoon crushed red pepper flakes

2 teaspoons liquid smoke

12 burger buns, split

½ pint (1 cup) creamy coleslaw (from deli)

1. Spray 4- to 6-quart slow cooker with cooking spray. In slow cooker, place turkey thighs. In small bowl, mix remaining ingredients except buns and coleslaw. Pour over turkey, turning turkey as necessary to coat.

2. Cover; cook on Low heat setting 8 to 10 hours.

3. Remove turkey from slow cooker; place on cutting board. Remove meat from bones; discard bones. Shred turkey with 2 forks; return to slow cooker and mix well.

4. To serve, with slotted spoon, spoon about ⅓ cup turkey mixture onto bottom halves of buns. Top each with rounded tablespoon coleslaw. Cover with top halves of buns.

1 Sandwich: Calories 340; Total Fat 9g (Saturated Fat 2.5g; Trans Fat 0g); Cholesterol 105mg; Sodium 610mg; Total Carbohydrate 33g (Dietary Fiber 1g) **Exchanges:** 1½ Starch, ½ Other Carbohydrate, 3½ Very Lean Meat, 1½ Fat **Carbohydrate Choices:** 2

QuickTip

For a real southern treat, serve this barbecued turkey over warm baking powder biscuits. Just pop some refrigerated baking powder biscuits into the oven while you shred the turkey.

Tex-Mex Wraps with Turkey

2 lb turkey breast tenderloins

¼ teaspoon seasoned salt

¼ teaspoon pepper

1 medium onion, chopped (½ cup)

⅓ cup water

2 packages (1.25 oz each) taco
   seasoning mix

16 flour tortillas (8 to 10 inch)

2 cups bite-sized pieces lettuce

2 cups shredded Cheddar
   cheese (8 oz)

1. In 3½- to 4-quart slow cooker, place turkey breast tenderloins. Sprinkle with seasoned salt and pepper. Add onion and water.

2. Cover; cook on Low heat setting 6 to 7 hours.

3. Remove turkey from slow cooker; place on cutting board. Shred turkey with 2 forks. Measure liquid from slow cooker; add enough water to liquid to measure 2 cups. Return liquid to slow cooker. Add taco seasoning mix; mix well. Stir in shredded turkey. Cover; cook on Low heat setting 1 hour longer.

4. To serve, spoon about ¼ cup turkey onto center of each tortilla. Top each with lettuce and cheese; roll up.

1 Sandwich: Calories 270; Total Fat 9g (Saturated Fat 4g; Trans Fat 0.5g); Cholesterol 50mg; Sodium 610mg; Total Carbohydrate 28g (Dietary Fiber 1g) **Exchanges:** 1 Starch, 1 Other Carbohydrate, 2½ Lean Meat **Carbohydrate Choices:** 2

QuickTip

If you're making these wraps to go, pack the lettuce, tortillas and cheese in separate containers and take the turkey in the slow cooker. If there's electricity at the site, plug in the cooker and set it on Low; otherwise, serve the sandwiches within an hour.

Turkey Teriyaki Sandwiches

2 bone-in turkey thighs (1½ lb), skin removed

½ cup teriyaki baste and glaze

2 tablespoons orange marmalade

½ teaspoon grated gingerroot

1 clove garlic, finely chopped

1 tablespoon water

2 teaspoons cornstarch

4 kaiser rolls, split

1. Spray 3½- or 4-quart slow cooker with cooking spray. In slow cooker, place turkey thighs. In small bowl or measuring cup, mix teriyaki baste and glaze, marmalade, gingerroot and garlic. Spoon mixture over turkey, turning as necessary to coat.

2. Cover; cook on Low heat setting 9 to 10 hours.

3. Remove turkey from slow cooker; place on cutting board. Remove and discard bones; shred or cut turkey into pieces.

4. In 2-cup glass measuring cup or small microwavable bowl, mix water and cornstarch until smooth. Pour juices from slow cooker into cornstarch mixture; mix well. Microwave uncovered on High 1 to 2 minutes or until mixture boils and thickens slightly, stirring once halfway through cooking.

5. To serve, spoon turkey onto bottom half of each roll; spoon sauce over turkey. Cover with top halves of rolls.

1 Sandwich: Calories 370; Total Fat 6g (Saturated Fat 1.5g; Trans Fat 0.5g); Cholesterol 105mg; Sodium 1160mg; Total Carbohydrate 46g (Dietary Fiber 1g) **Exchanges:** 2 Starch, 1 Other Carbohydrate, 4 Very Lean Meat, ½ Fat **Carbohydrate Choices:** 3

prep time
15 minutes

start to finish
4 hours 15 minutes

slow cooker
3½ to 4 quart

12 sandwiches

Italian Ground Turkey Rolls

1 teaspoon vegetable oil

2½ lb lean (at least 90%)
    ground turkey

1 medium onion, chopped (½ cup)

3 to 4 cloves garlic, finely chopped

1 jar (48 oz) chunky garden
    vegetable tomato pasta sauce

1 can (6 oz) tomato paste

12 French rolls (6 inch), split

6 slices (1½ oz each) mozzarella
    cheese, halved

1. In 10-inch nonstick skillet, heat oil over medium-high heat until hot. Cook turkey, onion and garlic in oil 6 to 8 minutes, stirring frequently, until turkey is well browned; drain.

2. In 3½- to 4-quart slow cooker, mix cooked turkey mixture, pasta sauce and tomato paste.

3. Cover; cook on Low heat setting 4 to 5 hours or on High heat setting 2 hours.

4. To serve, spoon ½ cup turkey mixture onto bottom halves of rolls. Top each with half slice of cheese, cutting to fit. Cover with top halves of rolls.

1 Sandwich: Calories 430; Total Fat 12g (Saturated Fat 4.5g; Trans Fat 0g); Cholesterol 75mg; Sodium 970mg; Total Carbohydrate 46g (Dietary Fiber 4g) **Exchanges:** 2 Starch, 1 Other Carbohydrate, 4 Lean Meat **Carbohydrate Choices:** 3

prep time
15 minutes

start to finish
10 hours 15 minutes

slow cooker
3½ to 4 quart

10 servings

Open-Faced Italian Brisket Sandwiches

3 lb fresh beef brisket (not corned beef), partially frozen

1 medium onion, quartered, sliced

1 can (19 oz) ready-to-serve tomato basil or hearty tomato soup

2 tablespoons cornstarch

2 tablespoons packed brown sugar

½ teaspoon Italian seasoning

⅛ teaspoon ground red pepper (cayenne)

2 tablespoons Worcestershire sauce

10 slices (½ inch thick) Italian bread

10 slices (1 oz each) provolone cheese

2 tablespoons chopped fresh parsley

1. Cut beef diagonally across grain into thin slices. In 3½- or 4-quart slow cooker, place beef. Add onion.

2. In medium bowl, mix soup, cornstarch, brown sugar, Italian seasoning, red pepper and Worcestershire sauce until smooth. Pour over beef and onion.

3. Cover; cook on Low heat setting 10 to 12 hours.

4. To serve, place 1 slice of bread on each individual plate. Top each with slice of cheese. Spoon about ¾ cup beef mixture over each. Sprinkle with parsley.

1 Serving: Calories 410; Total Fat 18g (Saturated Fat 8g; Trans Fat 0.5g); Cholesterol 75mg; Sodium 650mg; Total Carbohydrate 23g (Dietary Fiber 1g) Exchanges: 1 Starch, ½ Other Carbohydrate, 5 Lean Meat, ½ Fat Carbohydrate Choices: 1½

Beef Au Jus Sandwiches

1 large sweet onion, sliced

1 can (14 oz) beef broth

4 lb boneless beef rump roast, trimmed of fat

2 tablespoons balsamic vinegar

1 package (0.7 oz) Italian dressing mix

½ teaspoon salt

¼ teaspoon freshly ground black pepper

12 hoagie buns, split

1 large green bell pepper, thinly sliced

12 slices (1 oz each) provolone cheese, halved

1. In 3½- to 4-quart slow cooker, place onion slices and broth. Brush all surfaces of beef roast with vinegar. Place on onions. Sprinkle with dressing mix, salt and pepper.

2. Cover; cook on Low heat setting 8 to 10 hours.

3. Remove beef from slow cooker; place on cutting board. Cut beef across grain into thin slices; return slices to slow cooker, and mix well.

4. To serve, spoon beef onto bottom halves of buns. Top with bell pepper, cheese and top halves of buns. Serve sandwiches with juices from slow cooker.

1 Sandwich: Calories 550; Total Fat 16g (Saturated Fat 7g; Trans Fat 1g); Cholesterol 100mg; Sodium 1190mg; Total Carbohydrate 50g (Dietary Fiber 2g) Exchanges: 2½ Starch, 1 Other Carbohydrate, 6 Very Lean Meat, 2 Fat Carbohydrate Choices: 3

QuickTip

For a quick flavor-boost, serve horseradish sauce, barbecue sauce or a hearty grain mustard to top these already tasty beef sandwiches.

Double-Onion Beef Sandwiches

3 large cloves garlic, finely chopped

1 tablespoon Worcestershire sauce

½ teaspoon coarsely ground black pepper

3 lb fresh beef brisket (not corned beef)

1 medium onion, thinly sliced

1 package (1.3 oz) onion soup mix

½ cup water

8 individual French rolls or crusty rolls

1. In small bowl, mix garlic, Worcestershire sauce and pepper. Rub on both sides of beef brisket. Cut beef in half or thirds to fit slow cooker. In 3½- to 6-quart slow cooker, place sliced onion. Top with beef pieces. Sprinkle with soup mix. Add water.

2. Cover; cook on Low heat setting 8 to 10 hours.

3. Remove beef from slow cooker; place on cutting board. Cut beef across grain into thin slices. Skim fat from juices in slow cooker. Return beef to slow cooker; mix well.

4. To serve, cut rolls horizontally in half. Spoon beef mixture onto bottom halves of rolls. Drizzle with juices. Cover with top halves of rolls.

1 Sandwich: Calories 400; Total Fat 12g (Saturated Fat 4.5g; Trans Fat 0.5g); Cholesterol 70mg; Sodium 760mg; Total Carbohydrate 31g (Dietary Fiber 1g) Exchanges: 1½ Starch, ½ Other Carbohydrate, 5 Very Lean Meat, 1½ Fat Carbohydrate Choices: 2

QuickTip

Save yourself the time of chopping by picking up a jar of chopped garlic. When a recipe calls for a clove of garlic, you'll need ½ teaspoon chopped garlic.

Tangy Barbecued Beef Sandwiches

3½ to 4 lb boneless beef chuck roast, cut crosswise into ¼-inch slices

1¾ cups ketchup

½ cup packed brown sugar

⅓ cup vinegar

⅓ cup Worcestershire sauce

1 large onion, chopped (1 cup)

4 cloves garlic, finely chopped

3 tablespoons lemon juice

2 teaspoons ground mustard

1 teaspoon chili powder

1 teaspoon paprika

22 burger buns, split

1. In 3- to 4-quart slow cooker, mix all ingredients except buns.

2. Cover; cook on Low heat setting 5 to 6 hours, stirring occasionally.

3. To serve, cut off top of each bun; pull some of bread out of each bun. Fill buns with beef mixture.

1 Sandwich: Calories 300; Total Fat 11g (Saturated Fat 3.5g; Trans Fat 0.5g); Cholesterol 40mg; Sodium 500mg; Total Carbohydrate 33g (Dietary Fiber 1g) **Exchanges:** 1 Starch, 1 Other Carbohydrate, 2 Lean Meat, 1 Fat **Carbohydrate Choices:** 2

QuickTip

Slicing the beef is a snap if you freeze it 20 to 30 minutes or until it's firm but not frozen.

Smoky Barbecued Beef Sandwiches

2½ lb lean (at least 80%) ground beef

1½ cups barbecue sauce

⅓ cup teriyaki baste and glaze sauce

1 tablespoon finely chopped chipotle chiles in adobo sauce (from 7-oz can)

1 teaspoon salt

10 soft hoagie buns (6 to 7 inch), split

1. In 12-inch nonstick skillet or Dutch oven, cook beef over medium heat 8 to 10 minutes, stirring occasionally, until thoroughly cooked; drain well.

2. In 3½- to 4-quart slow cooker, mix beef and remaining ingredients except buns.

3. Cover; cook on Low heat setting 4 to 6 hours.

4. To serve, stir beef mixture. Spoon ½ cup beef mixture into each bun.

1 Sandwich: Calories 380; Total Fat 15g (Saturated Fat 5g; Trans Fat 1g); Cholesterol 70mg; Sodium 1090mg; Total Carbohydrate 38g (Dietary Fiber 1g) **Exchanges:** 1½ Starch, 1 Other Carbohydrate, 2½ Medium-Fat Meat, ½ Fat **Carbohydrate Choices:** 2½

QuickTip

Refrigerate the remaining chipotle chiles to add zip to chili, stew, beans or eggs. For extended storage, spoon chiles into a quart-sized resealable freezer plastic bag.

Southern Barbecued Beef Sandwiches

4 lb boneless beef round steak, ¾ inch thick, trimmed of fat, cut into pieces

2 cups ketchup

1 cup cola carbonated beverage

1 tablespoon prepared horseradish

2 cloves garlic, finely chopped

1 medium onion, chopped (½ cup)

24 burger buns, split

1. In 3½- to 4-quart slow cooker, arrange beef. Add remaining ingredients except buns; mix well.

2. Cover; cook on High heat setting 5 to 6 hours.

3. Remove beef from slow cooker; place on cutting board. Shred beef with 2 forks; return to slow cooker, and mix well. Cover; cook about 20 minutes longer or until beef is moistened and hot.

4. To serve, with slotted spoon, spoon about ⅓ cup beef mixture into each bun. Mixture can be kept warm for several hours on Low heat setting.

1 Sandwich: Calories 260; Total Fat 5g (Saturated Fat 1.5g; Trans Fat 0g); Cholesterol 55mg; Sodium 460mg; Total Carbohydrate 28g (Dietary Fiber 1g) **Exchanges:** 1½ Starch, ½ Other Carbohydrate, 3 Very Lean Meat, ½ Fat **Carbohydrate Choices:** 2

QuickTip

Barbecued beef is great to have on hand for a quick meal. Place the cooked beef in pint-sized freezer containers, and freeze up to four months. To thaw, place in the refrigerator for about eight hours, then reheat in a saucepan or in the microwave.

Sloppy Joes

3 lb lean (at least 80%) ground beef

1 large onion, chopped (1 cup)

2 medium stalks celery, chopped (1 cup)

½ cup chopped green bell pepper

1 bottle (12 oz) chili sauce

1 can (6 oz) tomato paste

2 to 3 tablespoons packed brown sugar

2 tablespoons Worcestershire sauce

¼ teaspoon pepper

16 burger buns, split

1. In 12-inch skillet or Dutch oven, cook beef, onion, celery and bell pepper over medium-high heat 5 to 7 minutes, stirring frequently, until beef is thoroughly cooked; drain.

2. In 3½- to 4-quart slow cooker, mix beef mixture and remaining ingredients except buns.

3. Cover; cook on Low heat setting 4 to 6 hours.

4. To serve, stir beef mixture. Spoon beef mixture into buns.

1 Sandwich: Calories 310; Total Fat 11g (Saturated Fat 4g; Trans Fat 1g); Cholesterol 55mg; Sodium 640mg; Total Carbohydrate 31g (Dietary Fiber 3g) **Exchanges:** 1½ Starch, ½ Other Carbohydrate, 2 Medium-Fat Meat **Carbohydrate Choices:** 2

QuickTip

Don't save time by omitting cooking the ground beef before adding it to the slow cooker. Due to the lower temperatures used in the slow cooker, it would be a food safety risk. Also, using cooked and drained ground beef helps eliminate the extra fat and liquid that would accumulate during cooking.

Barbecued Shredded Pork Sandwiches

½ cup barbecue sauce

½ cup sweet-and-sour sauce

1 clove garlic, finely chopped

2 lb boneless country-style pork ribs, trimmed of fat, cut into 2-inch pieces

6 kaiser rolls, split

1. In 3½- to 4-quart slow cooker, mix both sauces and the garlic. Stir in pork to coat.

2. Cover; cook on Low heat setting 8 to 10 hours.

3. Remove pork from slow cooker; place on cutting board. Shred pork by pulling apart with 2 forks. Return pork to sauce in slow cooker; mix well.

4. To serve, spoon about ½ cup pork mixture into each roll.

1 Sandwich: Calories 490; Total Fat 20g (Saturated Fat 7g; Trans Fat 0.5g); Cholesterol 95mg; Sodium 630mg; Total Carbohydrate 41g (Dietary Fiber 1g) **Exchanges:** 1½ Starch, 1 Other Carbohydrate, 4 Medium-Fat Meat **Carbohydrate Choices:** 3

Spicy Pulled Pork Sandwiches

3 lb boneless pork shoulder or butt roast, trimmed of fat

¼ cup packed brown sugar

2 teaspoons dried thyme leaves

1 teaspoon salt

2 teaspoons red pepper sauce

2 cloves garlic, finely chopped

1 can (6 oz) tomato paste

1 can (4.5 oz) chopped green chiles

12 burger buns, split

½ pint (1 cup) creamy coleslaw (from deli)

1. In 3½- to 4-quart slow cooker, place pork roast. In small bowl, mix brown sugar, thyme, salt, pepper sauce, garlic, tomato paste and chiles. Spread over pork.

2. Cover; cook on Low heat setting 8 to 9 hours.

3. Just before serving, remove pork from slow cooker; place on cutting board. Shred pork with 2 forks; return to slow cooker, and mix well.

4. To serve, spoon ½ cup pork mixture on bottom half of each bun. Top each with rounded tablespoon coleslaw. Cover with top halves of buns.

1 Sandwich: Calories 340; Total Fat 15g (Saturated Fat 4.5g; Trans Fat 0g); Cholesterol 50mg; Sodium 620mg; Total Carbohydrate 30g (Dietary Fiber 2g) Exchanges: 1 Starch, 1 Other Carbohydrate, 2½ Lean Meat, 1½ Fat Carbohydrate Choices: 2

QuickTip

Use ½ teaspoon purchased chopped garlic (from a jar) in place of the garlic cloves. Store the opened jar of garlic in the refrigerator.

Sweet-and-Saucy Ham Sandwiches

1½ lb cooked smoked ham, ground (4 cups)

1 cup packed brown sugar

½ cup Dijon mustard

¼ cup chopped green bell pepper

1 tablespoon instant minced onion

1 can (20 oz) crushed pineapple in juice, undrained

12 burger buns, split

1. In 3½- to 6-quart slow cooker, mix all ingredients except buns.

2. Cover; cook on Low heat setting 3 to 4 hours.

3. Remove cover from slow cooker. Increase heat setting to High; cook, uncovered, 10 to 15 minutes longer or until desired consistency.

4. To serve, stir ham mixture well; spoon into buns.

1 Sandwich: Calories 330; Total Fat 8g (Saturated Fat 2.5g; Trans Fat 0g); Cholesterol 35mg; Sodium 1310mg; Total Carbohydrate 48g (Dietary Fiber 1g) **Exchanges:** 1½ Starch, 1½ Other Carbohydrate, 2 Lean Meat **Carbohydrate Choices:** 3

QuickTip

If your butcher can't grind the ham for you, use a food processor to finely chop the ham instead of grinding it. Or finely chop the ham with a chef knife the night before to save time in the morning.

great sides & starters

Alfredo Green Bean Casserole

2 bags (1 lb each) frozen cut green beans

1 can (8 oz) sliced water chestnuts, drained

½ cup roasted red bell peppers (from a jar), cut into small strips

¼ teaspoon salt

1 container (10 oz) refrigerated Alfredo pasta sauce

1 can (2.8 oz) French-fried onions

1. Spray inside of 3- to 4-quart slow cooker with cooking spray. In large bowl, mix all ingredients except onions. Stir in half of the onions; spoon mixture into slow cooker.

2. Cover; cook on Low heat setting 3 to 4 hours, stirring after 1 to 1½ hours.

3. Just before serving, in 6-inch skillet, heat remaining half of onions over medium-high heat 2 to 3 minutes, stirring frequently, until hot. Stir bean mixture; sprinkle with onions.

1 Serving: Calories 190; Total Fat 13g (Saturated Fat 7g; Trans Fat 1.5g); Cholesterol 30mg; Sodium 240mg; Total Carbohydrate 13g (Dietary Fiber 3g) Exchanges: ½ Other Carbohydrate, 1½ Vegetable, 2½ Fat Carbohydrate Choices: 1

QuickTip

Either jarred Alfredo sauce or sauce prepared from a dry mix can be used. Whichever sauce you choose, measure 1¼ cups.

Scalloped Corn

⅔ cup all-purpose flour

¼ cup butter or margarine, melted

1 carton (8 oz) fat-free egg product (1 cup)

¾ cup evaporated milk

2 teaspoons sugar

1 teaspoon salt

⅛ teaspoon pepper

1 can (14.75 oz) cream-style corn

1 can (15.25 oz) whole kernel corn, drained

1. Spray 2- to 4-quart slow cooker with cooking spray. In large bowl, mix all ingredients except whole kernel corn. Stir in whole kernel corn. Pour into slow cooker.

2. Cover; cook on High heat setting 2 to 3 hours.

1 Serving: Calories 240; Total Fat 9g (Saturated Fat 5g; Trans Fat 0g); Cholesterol 20mg; Sodium 730mg; Total Carbohydrate 31g (Dietary Fiber 2g) **Exchanges:** 2 Starch, 1½ Fat **Carbohydrate Choices:** 2

QuickTip

If you like, use four eggs instead of the fat-free egg product. Beat the eggs using a fork or whisk before adding to the other ingredients.

Cheesy Winter Vegetables Casserole

1 bag (20 oz) refrigerated cooked new potato wedges

1 bag (16 oz) ready-to-eat baby-cut carrots

1 medium stalk celery, cut into 1-inch pieces (½ cup)

1 can (10¾ oz) condensed Cheddar cheese soup

2 teaspoons Worcestershire sauce

⅛ teaspoon ground red pepper (cayenne), if desired

1 cup frozen sweet peas, thawed

1 cup shredded American-Cheddar cheese blend (4 oz)

1. In 3½- to 4-quart slow cooker, mix potatoes, carrots and celery. In small bowl, mix soup, Worcestershire sauce and red pepper. Pour soup mixture over vegetables; stir gently to coat.

2. Cover; cook on Low heat setting 6 to 7 hours.

3. Gently stir thawed peas and cheese into vegetable mixture. Cover; cook about 10 minutes longer or until peas are tender.

1 Serving: Calories 120; Total Fat 5g (Saturated Fat 3g; Trans Fat 0g); Cholesterol 15mg; Sodium 380mg; Total Carbohydrate 13g (Dietary Fiber 2g) Exchanges: ½ Starch, 1 Vegetable, 1 Fat Carbohydrate Choices: 1

Vegetable-Rice Pilaf

1 can (14 oz) chicken broth with roasted garlic

⅔ cup water

1½ cups uncooked converted long-grain white rice

1 tablespoon olive oil

1¼ cups frozen cut green beans

1 medium carrot, sliced (½ cup)

2 medium green onions, sliced (2 tablespoons)

½ teaspoon salt

¼ teaspoon lemon-pepper seasoning

1. In 4-cup glass measuring cup, mix broth and water. Microwave uncovered on High 4 to 5 minutes or until steaming hot.

2. Meanwhile, spray 4- to 6-quart slow cooker with cooking spray. In slow cooker, mix rice and oil. Add hot broth mixture and remaining ingredients.

3. Cover; cook on High heat setting 1½ to 2 hours.

1 Serving: Calories 110; Total Fat 1.5g (Saturated Fat 0g; Trans Fat 0g); Cholesterol 0mg; Sodium 250mg; Total Carbohydrate 21g (Dietary Fiber 0g) Exchanges: 1 Starch, ½ Other Carbohydrate Carbohydrate Choices: 1½

QuickTip

A can of chicken broth and ¼ teaspoon garlic powder can be used for the chicken broth with roasted garlic. And if you don't have lemon-pepper seasoning, use ¼ teaspoon black pepper, and if you like, stir in ¼ teaspoon grated lemon peel before serving.

Creamy Parmesan Potatoes

8 medium russet or Idaho potatoes, peeled, sliced (about 3 lb)

1 can (10¾ oz) condensed golden mushroom soup

½ cup water

¼ cup all-purpose flour

3 tablespoons butter or margarine, melted

½ teaspoon salt

¼ teaspoon pepper

¼ teaspoon garlic powder

⅓ cup shredded fresh Parmesan cheese, if desired

1. In 3- to 4-quart slow cooker, place potatoes. In medium bowl, mix soup, water, flour, butter, salt, pepper and garlic powder. Pour mixture over potatoes; stir gently to coat.

2. Cover; cook on Low heat setting 5 to 6 hours.

3. Just before serving, sprinkle Parmesan cheese over top.

1 Serving: Calories 160; Total Fat 4.5g (Saturated Fat 2g; Trans Fat 0g); Cholesterol 10mg; Sodium 300mg; Total Carbohydrate 26g (Dietary Fiber 2g) **Exchanges:** 1 Starch, ½ Other Carbohydrate, 1 Fat **Carbohydrate Choices:** 2

QuickTip

If you like mushrooms, stir in a six-ounce jar of sliced mushrooms, drained, with the soup.

Au Gratin Potatoes and Onion

6 medium russet or Idaho potatoes, peeled, sliced (about 2¼ lb)

1 medium onion, coarsely chopped (½ cup)

1 cup shredded American cheese (4 oz)

1 can (10¾ oz) condensed 98% fat-free cream of mushroom soup with 30% less sodium

½ cup milk

¼ to ½ teaspoon dried thyme leaves

1. In 3½-quart slow cooker, layer half each of the potatoes, onion and cheese; repeat layers. In small bowl, mix soup, milk and thyme. Pour over potatoes in slow cooker.

2. Cover; cook on High heat setting 1 hour. Reduce heat setting to Low. Cook 6 to 8 hours longer.

1 Serving: Calories 110; Total Fat 3.5g (Saturated Fat 2g; Trans Fat 0g); Cholesterol 10mg; Sodium 210mg; Total Carbohydrate 16g (Dietary Fiber 1g) **Exchanges:** 1 Starch, ½ Fat **Carbohydrate Choices:** 1

QuickTip

Regular cream of mushroom soup can be used as well as other cream soups such as cream of chicken or cream of celery soup.

Garlic Smashed Red Potatoes

3 lb small red potatoes (2 to 3 inch)

4 cloves garlic, finely chopped

1 teaspoon salt

½ cup water

2 tablespoons olive oil

½ cup chives-and-onion cream cheese spread (from 8-oz container)

½ to ¾ cup milk

1. Cut potatoes into halves or quarters as necessary to make similar-sized pieces. In 4- to 6-quart slow cooker, place potatoes. Stir in garlic, salt, water and oil until potato pieces are coated.

2. Cover; cook on High heat setting 3½ to 4½ hours or until potatoes are tender.

3. With fork or potato masher, mash potatoes and garlic. Stir in cream cheese spread until well blended. Stir in enough milk for soft serving consistency. Serve immediately, or cover and hold in slow cooker on Low heat setting up to 2 hours.

1 Serving: Calories 120; Total Fat 4.5g (Saturated Fat 2g; Trans Fat 0g); Cholesterol 10mg; Sodium 240mg; Total Carbohydrate 18g (Dietary Fiber 2g) **Exchanges:** 1 Starch, 1 Fat **Carbohydrate Choices:** 1

Chile-Cheese Party Potatoes

1 can (10¾ oz) condensed cream of mushroom soup

1 container (8 oz) sour cream

1 can (4.5 oz) chopped green chiles

1½ cups shredded Colby-Monterey Jack cheese blend (6 oz)

1 bag (32 oz) frozen southern-style diced hash brown potatoes

3 medium green onions, sliced (3 tablespoons)

½ cup finely crushed nacho-flavored tortilla chips

1. Spray 4- to 6-quart slow cooker with cooking spray. In medium bowl, mix soup, sour cream, chiles and cheese.

2. In slow cooker, arrange half of the potatoes. Top with half of sour cream mixture; spread evenly. Top with remaining potatoes and sour cream mixture; spread evenly.

3. Cover; cook on High heat setting 3½ to 4½ hours. Sprinkle onions and chips onto potato mixture before serving.

1 Serving: Calories 230; Total Fat 11g (Saturated Fat 6g; Trans Fat 0g); Cholesterol 25mg; Sodium 350mg; Total Carbohydrate 27g (Dietary Fiber 2g) Exchanges: 1½ Starch, ½ Other Carbohydrate, 2 Fat Carbohydrate Choices: 2

QuickTip

Southern-style hash brown potatoes are diced and the country-style hash browns are shredded. This recipe calls for diced potatoes, but both styles work well.

Southwestern Calico Baked Beans

1 package (12 oz) bulk spicy pork sausage

1 can (55 oz) or 4 cans (15 oz each) baked beans, drained

1 can (15.5 or 15 oz) dark red kidney beans, drained

1 can (15 oz) black-eyed peas, drained

1 box (9 oz) frozen baby lima beans

1 cup chunky-style salsa

1 package (1.25 oz) taco seasoning mix

1. In 8-inch skillet, cook sausage over medium heat, stirring frequently, until no longer pink; drain.

2. In 3½- or 4-quart slow cooker, gently mix cooked sausage and remaining ingredients.

3. Cover; cook on Low heat setting 5 to 6 hours.

1 Serving: Calories 170; Total Fat 3.5g (Saturated Fat 1g; Trans Fat 0g); Cholesterol 10mg; Sodium 630mg; Total Carbohydrate 26g (Dietary Fiber 7g) **Exchanges:** 1 Starch, ½ Other Carbohydrate, 1 Lean Meat **Carbohydrate Choices:** 2

Texas-Style Barbecued Beans

6 slices bacon

4 cans (15.5 oz each) great northern beans, drained, rinsed

4 cans (15 oz each) black beans, drained, rinsed

4 cloves garlic, finely chopped

¾ cup finely chopped onion

1½ cups ketchup

½ cup packed brown sugar

½ cup barbecue sauce

2 tablespoons yellow mustard

2 tablespoons Worcestershire sauce

3 teaspoons chili powder

½ teaspoon red pepper sauce

1. In 10-inch skillet, cook bacon over medium heat until crisp. Remove bacon from skillet; drain on paper towels.

2. In 3½- or 4-quart slow cooker, gently mix all ingredients except bacon. Crumble bacon; sprinkle over bean mixture.

3. Cover; cook on Low heat setting 4 to 6 hours.

1 Serving: Calories 240; Total Fat 1.5g (Saturated Fat 0g; Trans Fat 0g); Cholesterol 0mg; Sodium 310mg; Total Carbohydrate 43g (Dietary Fiber 10g) **Exchanges:** 1½ Starch, 1½ Other Carbohydrate, 1 Very Lean Meat **Carbohydrate Choices:** 3

QuickTip

Too much red pepper sauce can become bitter during long slow cooking. Taste the beans before serving and stir in more red pepper sauce if you like spicier beans. You can use ½ teaspoon garlic powder instead of chopping fresh garlic.

Creamy Wild Rice

1½ cups uncooked wild rice

1 medium onion, chopped (½ cup)

½ teaspoon salt

½ teaspoon ground sage

¼ teaspoon pepper

1 can (10¾ oz) condensed cream of
   celery soup

1 can (10¾ oz) condensed cream of
   mushroom soup

2¼ cups water

¼ cup chopped fresh parsley

1. Rinse rice with cold water; drain. In 5- to 6-quart slow cooker, mix rice and all remaining ingredients except parsley.

2. Cover; cook on Low heat setting 8 to 9 hours. Stir in parsley before serving.

1 Serving: Calories 130; Total Fat 3.5g (Saturated Fat 1g; Trans Fat 0g); Cholesterol 0mg; Sodium 460mg; Total Carbohydrate 22g (Dietary Fiber 2g) **Exchanges:** 1 Starch, ½ Other Carbohydrate, ½ Fat **Carbohydrate Choices:** 1½

QuickTip

To add crunch to this creamy dish, add a couple tablespoons of toasted pecans or almonds before serving. You can either stir them in or sprinkle them right on top.

Apple-Walnut Stuffing

½ cup butter or margarine

½ cup chopped walnuts

1 tablespoon honey

⅛ teaspoon ground nutmeg

2 medium stalks celery, sliced
(1 cup)

1 large onion, chopped (1 cup)

1 package (14 oz) herb-seasoned
stuffing cubes

1 jar (4.5 oz) sliced mushrooms,
drained

1½ cups applesauce

2 cups water

1. In 8-inch skillet, heat 2 tablespoons of the butter and the walnuts over medium heat, stirring occasionally, until nuts are lightly toasted. With slotted spoon, remove nuts from skillet; place in small dish. Add honey and nutmeg to nuts; mix to glaze. Set aside.

2. In same skillet, melt remaining 6 tablespoons butter over medium heat. Cook celery and onion in butter over medium heat 3 to 4 minutes, stirring occasionally, until almost tender.

3. Meanwhile, spray 4- to 6-quart slow cooker with cooking spray. In slow cooker, place stuffing cubes. Add mushrooms and celery mixture; mix lightly. Add applesauce and water; mix lightly.

4. Cover; cook on Low heat setting 4 to 5 hours.

5. Just before serving, sprinkle with glazed walnuts.

1 Serving: Calories 320; Total Fat 15g (Saturated Fat 7g; Trans Fat 0.5g); Cholesterol 25mg; Sodium 750mg; Total Carbohydrate 43g (Dietary Fiber 3g) **Exchanges:** 1½ Starch, 1½ Other Carbohydrate, 2½ Fat **Carbohydrate Choices:** 3

QuickTip

This stuffing will be moist. If you prefer a drier stuffing, reduce the water to 1½ cups. For a flavor change, make apple-sausage stuffing. Omit the walnuts and reduce the butter to ¼ cup. Add 12 oz cooked and drained sausage with the mushrooms.

Winter Fruit Compote

1 two-inch cinnamon stick

2 small apples, peeled, sliced

⅓ cup sweetened dried cranberries

½ cup golden raisins

½ cup halved dried apricots

1 can (8 oz) pineapple tidbits in juice, undrained

¼ cup sugar

¾ cup orange juice

1 can (21 oz) peach pie filling

1. In 1½- to 2½-quart slow cooker, place cinnamon stick. Layer with apples, cranberries, raisins, apricots and pineapple with juice. Sprinkle with sugar. Pour orange juice over top.

2. Cover; cook on Low heat setting 5 to 6 hours.

3. Just before serving, gently stir mixture. Remove and discard cinnamon stick. Gently stir in pie filling, cutting peach slices into smaller pieces as necessary.

1 Serving: Calories 270; Total Fat 0g (Saturated Fat 0g; Trans Fat 0g); Cholesterol 0mg; Sodium 20mg; Total Carbohydrate 67g (Dietary Fiber 2g) **Exchanges:** 1 Fruit, 3½ Other Carbohydrate **Carbohydrate Choices:** 4½

QuickTip

Prepared pie filling helps thicken this slow-cooked recipe. It is added shortly before serving to retain its pretty color and texture. If you like, you can use a can of apple pie filling for the peach pie filling.

Caesar Artichoke Dip

1 can (14 oz) quartered artichoke hearts, drained, coarsely chopped

1 package (8 oz) cream cheese, cut into cubes

½ cup creamy Caesar dressing

¾ cup shredded Parmesan cheese (3 oz)

4 medium green onions, chopped (¼ cup)

Dash red pepper sauce

Additional chopped green onions, if desired

Toasted bread slices or crisp flat crackers, if desired

1. Spray inside of 1- to 1½-quart slow cooker with cooking spray. In slow cooker, mix all ingredients except additional green onions and crackers.

2. Cover; cook on Low heat setting 2 to 3 hours or until hot.

3. Before serving, stir until dip is well blended and smooth. Top with green onions. Serve with bread slices. Dip can be held on Low heat setting up to 1 hour.

1 Serving (2 tablespoons dip): Calories 100; Total Fat 8g (Saturated Fat 3.5g; Trans Fat 0g); Cholesterol 15mg; Sodium 210mg; Total Carbohydrate 2g (Dietary Fiber 0g) **Exchanges:** ½ High-Fat Meat, 1 Fat **Carbohydrate Choices:** 0

Pizza Dip

¾ lb bulk Italian pork sausage

1 small onion, chopped (¼ cup)

½ cup sliced pepperoni, chopped (2 oz)

¼ cup ketchup

1 jar (14 oz) pizza sauce

2 cups shredded mozzarella cheese (8 oz)

1 loaf (16 inch) baguette French bread, cut into 56 thin slices

1. In 10-inch skillet, cook sausage and onion over medium-high heat, stirring frequently, until sausage is no longer pink; drain. Stir in pepperoni, ketchup and pizza sauce.

2. Spray 1½- to 3-quart slow cooker with cooking spray. Spoon sausage mixture into slow cooker. Stir in cheese.

3. Cover; cook on Low heat setting 2 to 3 hours.

4. Stir dip before serving. Serve with bread slices.

1 Serving (2 tablespoons dip and 2 bread slices): Calories 110; Total Fat 4.5g (Saturated Fat 2g; Trans Fat 0g); Cholesterol 10mg; Sodium 280mg; Total Carbohydrate 12g (Dietary Fiber 0g) **Exchanges:** ½ Starch, ½ Other Carbohydrate, ½ High-Fat Meat **Carbohydrate Choices:** 1

QuickTip

Instead of slices of baguette, toast slices of bread and cut into triangles to serve with the dip.

Hot Reuben Spread

2 cups shredded Swiss cheese (8 oz)

¾ cup Thousand Island dressing

½ lb sliced cooked corned beef, coarsely chopped

1 can (16 oz) sauerkraut, rinsed, well drained

1 package (3 oz) cream cheese, cubed

Cocktail rye bread slices, toasted, if desired

1. In 1½- to 3-quart slow cooker, mix all ingredients except bread.

2. Cover; cook on Low heat setting 1½ to 2½ hours.

3. Stir spread before serving. Serve with toasted bread slices.

1 Serving (2 tablespoons spread): Calories 80; Total Fat 6g (Saturated Fat 2.5g; Trans Fat 0g); Cholesterol 15mg; Sodium 240mg; Total Carbohydrate 1g (Dietary Fiber 0g) **Exchanges:** ½ High-Fat Meat, ½ Fat **Carbohydrate Choices:** 0

QuickTip

This spread blends all the characteristic flavors of the Reuben Grill, a New York deli sandwich, into a luscious warm dip. Brighten the finished dip with a garnish of curly parsley.

Hot Artichoke and Spinach Dip

1 can (14 oz) quartered artichoke hearts, drained, chopped

1 box (9 oz) frozen spinach, thawed, squeezed to drain

1 cup shredded Swiss cheese (4 oz)

½ cup refrigerated Alfredo pasta sauce (from 10-oz container)

½ cup mayonnaise or salad dressing

¾ teaspoon garlic salt

¼ teaspoon pepper

1 loaf (20 inch) baguette French bread, cut into 40 slices

1. In 1- to 1½-quart slow cooker, mix all ingredients except bread.

2. Cover; cook on Low heat setting 2 to 4 hours. Serve dip with sliced bread.

1 Serving (2 tablespoons dip and 2 bread slices): Calories 130; Total Fat 8g (Saturated Fat 3g; Trans Fat 0g); Cholesterol 15mg; Sodium 240mg; Total Carbohydrate 10g (Dietary Fiber 2g) **Exchanges:** ½ Starch, ½ High-Fat Meat, 1 Fat **Carbohydrate Choices:** ½

QuickTip

You can use jarred Alfredo sauce, found with the other shelf-stable pasta sauces, in place of the refrigerated sauce.

Spicy Oriental Barbecued Chicken Drummettes

DRUMMETTES

1 package (3 lb) frozen chicken drummettes, thawed

2 tablespoons butter or margarine, melted

¼ cup all-purpose flour

SAUCE

⅓ cup hoisin sauce

2 tablespoons oriental chili garlic sauce

1 tablespoon butter or margarine, melted

1. Heat oven to 450°F. With paper towels, pat excess moisture from thawed drummettes. In large bowl, place drummettes. Drizzle with 2 tablespoons melted butter. Sprinkle with flour; toss to mix. (Mixture will be crumbly.) Transfer mixture to ungreased 15x10x1-inch baking pan, arranging drummettes in single layer.

2. Bake for 40 to 45 minutes or until crisp and brown.

3. With slotted spoon, transfer browned drummettes to 4- to 6-quart slow cooker. In small bowl, combine all sauce ingredients; mix well. Pour sauce over drummettes; toss lightly to coat with sauce.

4. Cover; cook on low setting for 1 to 2 hours.

1 Serving (2 drummettes): Calories 140; Total Fat 8g (Saturated Fat 2g; Trans Fat 1g); Cholesterol 40mg; Sodium 230mg; Total Carbohydrate 5g (Dietary Fiber 0g) **Exchanges:** ½ Other Carbohydrate, 2 Lean Meat **Carbohydrate Choices:** ½

QuickTip

Oriental chili garlic sauce, which is much hotter and thicker than traditional chili sauce, can be found in the Asian food section of the grocery store. For a milder flavor, use only one tablespoon of the sauce. Look for hoisin sauce in the Asian section of the store, too.

Shredded Chicken Nachos

NACHOS

2 lb boneless skinless chicken thighs (about 10)

1 package (1.25 oz) taco seasoning mix

1 can (15 oz) pinto beans, drained

1 can (14.5 oz) diced tomatoes, undrained

1 can (4.5 oz) chopped green chiles

2 tablespoons lime juice

10 oz restaurant-style tortilla chips (75 chips)

TOPPINGS

1 cup shredded Colby-Monterey Jack cheese blend (4 oz)

¾ cup sour cream

¾ cup chunky-style salsa

4 medium green onions, sliced (¼ cup)

¼ cup sliced ripe or green olives

2 tablespoons chopped fresh cilantro

1 lime, cut into 12 wedges

1. In 3½- to 4-quart slow cooker, place chicken thighs. Sprinkle with taco seasoning mix. Top with beans, tomatoes, chiles and lime juice.

2. Cover; cook on Low heat setting 7 to 8 hours.

3. Just before serving, place topping ingredients in individual serving dishes. Remove chicken from slow cooker; place on cutting board. Mash beans in slow cooker. Shred chicken with 2 forks; return to slow cooker and mix well.

4. To serve, have guests place chips on serving plates; spoon ½ cup chicken mixture onto chips. Top nachos with desired toppings. Chicken mixture can be held on Low heat setting up to 2 hours.

1 Serving: Calories 380; Total Fat 18g (Saturated Fat 6g; Trans Fat 0g); Cholesterol 65mg; Sodium 710mg; Total Carbohydrate 29g (Dietary Fiber 5g) **Exchanges:** 2 Starch, 2½ Lean Meat, 2 Fat **Carbohydrate Choices:** 2

QuickTip

You can serve these nachos on a large serving plate. Place half the tortilla chips on a plate and top with half the chicken mixture and half the toppings. Keep the chicken mixture warm in the slow cooker until you are ready to assemble the second plate. Or if you have a large platter, serve all the nachos at once.

Cheeseburger Bites

BITES

1 lb lean (at least 80%) ground beef

2 tablespoons ketchup

2 teaspoons instant minced onion

1 teaspoon yellow mustard

8 oz American cheese loaf, cut into
    2-inch cubes (2 cups)

24 miniature burger buns, split

TOPPINGS, AS DESIRED

Dill pickle chips

Sliced plum (Roma) tomatoes

Shredded lettuce

Additional ketchup and mustard

1. In 10-inch skillet, cook beef over medium-high heat 5 to 7 minutes, stirring frequently, until thoroughly cooked; drain. Stir in 2 tablespoons ketchup, the onion and 1 teaspoon mustard.

2. Spray 3½- to 4-quart slow cooker with cooking spray. Into slow cooker, spoon beef mixture. Top with cheese.

3. Cover; cook on Low heat setting 3 to 4 hours.

4. Just before serving, stir beef mixture. Spoon 1 rounded tablespoon mixture into each bun. Serve with desired toppings.

1 Appetizer (without Toppings): Calories 140; Total Fat 6g (Saturated Fat 3g; Trans Fat 0g); Cholesterol 20mg; Sodium 290mg; Total Carbohydrate 13g (Dietary Fiber 0g) **Exchanges:** 1 Starch, ½ Medium-Fat Meat, ½ Fat **Carbohydrate Choices:** 1

French Onion Meatballs

2 bags (18 oz each) frozen cooked original flavor meatballs

1 jar (12 oz) beef gravy

1 package (1 oz) onion soup mix (from 2-oz box)

1 tablespoon dry sherry, if desired

1. In 4- to 5-quart slow cooker, place meatballs. In medium bowl, mix gravy, soup mix and sherry; gently stir into meatballs.

2. Cover; cook on Low heat setting 3½ to 4½ hours.

3. Serve meatballs with fondue forks or long toothpicks. Meatballs can be held on Low heat setting up to 1 hour, with lid removed.

1 Serving: Calories 160; Total Fat 8g (Saturated Fat 3g; Trans Fat 0.5g); Cholesterol 60mg; Sodium 570mg; Total Carbohydrate 8g (Dietary Fiber 0g) **Exchanges:** ½ Starch, 1½ Medium-Fat Meat **Carbohydrate Choices:** ½

QuickTip

To make hearty meatball sandwiches, spoon the meatballs into split crusty rolls or buns. Serve with a crisp toss green salad for a quick evening meal.

prep time
10 minutes

start to finish
5 hours 10 minutes

slow cooker
3 to 3½ quart

16 servings

Bavarian Cocktail Meatballs

2 bags (16 oz each) frozen cooked
    meatballs (64 meatballs),
    thawed

1 medium onion, sliced

¼ cup packed brown sugar

3 tablespoons beefy onion soup mix
    (from 2.2-oz package)

1 can (12 oz) beer, or beef broth

1. In 3- or 3½-quart slow cooker, mix meatballs and onion. Sprinkle brown sugar and soup mix over beef and onion. Pour beer over top.

2. Cover; cook on Low heat setting 5 to 6 hours.

3. Just before serving, gently stir mixture to coat meatballs with sauce. Serve with long pretzel sticks or toothpicks. Meatballs can be held on Low heat setting up to 1 hour, with lid removed.

1 Serving: Calories 200; Total Fat 13g (Saturated Fat 5g; Trans Fat 0g); Cholesterol 30mg; Sodium 660mg; Total Carbohydrate 11g (Dietary Fiber 1g) Exchanges: 1 Other Carbohydrate, 1½ High-Fat Meat Carbohydrate Choices: 1

Curry-Mustard Glazed Meatballs

1 jar (12 oz) pineapple preserves

1 jar (8 oz) Dijon mustard

1 can (8 oz) pineapple tidbits in juice, undrained

½ cup packed dark brown sugar

1 teaspoon curry powder

2½ lb frozen cooked Italian-style meatballs (80 meatballs)

1. In 1-quart saucepan, mix all ingredients except meatballs. Heat to boiling. In 2½- to 3-quart slow cooker, place meatballs. Stir in preserves mixture.

2. Cover; cook on High heat setting 4 hours, stirring twice.

3. Just before serving, stir to coat meatballs with sauce. Serve with toothpicks. Meatballs can be held on Low heat setting up to 2 hours, with lid removed.

1 Serving (2 meatballs): Calories 130; Total Fat 7g (Saturated Fat 2.5g; Trans Fat 0g); Cholesterol 15mg; Sodium 310mg; Total Carbohydrate 12g (Dietary Fiber 0g) Exchanges: 1 Other Carbohydrate, ½ High-Fat Meat, ½ Fat Carbohydrate Choices: 1

Hot-and-Spicy Riblets

RIBLETS

1 rack (3 lb) pork back ribs, cut lengthwise in half across bones*, cut into 1-rib pieces

3 cloves garlic, finely chopped

SAUCE

1 cup ketchup

¼ cup packed brown sugar

¼ cup chopped chipotle chiles in adobo sauce

1 tablespoon cider vinegar

1 tablespoon Worcestershire sauce

1 teaspoon salt

1. Spray 3½- to 4-quart slow cooker with cooking spray. In slow cooker, place pork riblets. Sprinkle with garlic.

2. Cover; cook on Low heat setting 6 to 7 hours.

3. In 2-cup measuring cup or small bowl, mix sauce ingredients. Drain and discard juices from slow cooker. Pour or spoon sauce over riblets, stirring gently to coat evenly. Increase heat setting to High. Cover; cook 25 to 30 minutes longer or until riblets are glazed.

* Ask your butcher to cut the ribs lengthwise in half across the bone.

1 Serving: Calories 390; Total Fat 25g (Saturated Fat 9g; Trans Fat 0g); Cholesterol 100mg; Sodium 760mg; Total Carbohydrate 16g (Dietary Fiber 0g) **Exchanges:** 1 Other Carbohydrate, 3½ High-Fat Meat **Carbohydrate Choices:** 1

Mexican Chili Cheese Dogs

8 oz Mexican prepared cheese product with jalapeño peppers, cut into cubes (1½ cups)

½ cup mild taco sauce

1 can (15 oz) chili without beans

3 lb cocktail-sized hot dogs or smoked link sausages

¼ cup chopped fresh cilantro

1. In 3- to 4-quart slow cooker, place cheese, taco sauce, chili and hot dogs; stir to coat well.

2. Cover; cook on Low heat setting 5 to 6 hours, stirring once halfway through cook time.

3. Before serving, sprinkle with cilantro. Serve with toothpicks. Hot dogs can be held on Low heat setting up to 1 hour, with lid removed.

1 Serving: Calories 150; Total Fat 13g (Saturated Fat 5g; Trans Fat 0g); Cholesterol 30mg; Sodium 600mg; Total Carbohydrate 3g (Dietary Fiber 0g) **Exchanges:** 1 High-Fat Meat, 1 Fat **Carbohydrate Choices:** 0

QuickTip

You can use three pounds of regular-sized hot dogs for the cocktail sized. Cut them into about 1½-inch pieces.

helpful nutrition and cooking information

Nutrition Guidelines

We provide nutrition information for each recipe that includes calories, fat, cholesterol, sodium, carbohydrate, fiber exchanges and carbohydrate choices. Individual food choices can be based on this information.

Recommended Intake for a Daily Diet of 2,000 Calories as Set by the Food and Drug Administration

Total Fat	Less than 65g
Saturated Fat	Less than 20g
Cholesterol	Less than 300mg
Sodium	Less than 2,400mg
Total Carbohydrate	300g
Dietary Fiber	25g

Criteria Used for Calculating Nutrition Information

- The first ingredient was used wherever a choice is given (such as ⅓ cup sour cream or plain yogurt).

- The first ingredient amount was used wherever a range is given (such as 3- to 3½-pound cut-up broiler-fryer chicken).

- The first serving number was used wherever a range is given (such as 4 to 6 servings).

- "If desired" ingredients were not included (such as brown sugar, if desired).

- Only the amount of a marinade or frying oil that is estimated to be absorbed by the food during preparation or cooking was calculated.

Ingredients Used in Recipe Testing and Nutrition Calculations

- Ingredients used for testing represent those that the majority of consumers use in their homes: large eggs, 2% milk, 80%-lean ground beef and canned ready-to-use chicken broth.

- Fat-free, low-fat or low-sodium products were not used, unless otherwise indicated.

- Nonstick cooking sprays were used to grease slow cooker, unless otherwise indicated.

Equipment Used in Recipe Testing

We use equipment for testing that the majority of consumers use in their homes. If a specific piece of equipment (such as a wire whisk) is necessary for recipe success, it is listed in the recipe.

- Cookware and bakeware without nonstick coatings were used, unless otherwise indicated.
- No dark-colored, black or insulated bakeware was used.
- When a pan is specified in a recipe, a metal pan was used; a baking dish or pie plate means ovenproof glass was used.
- An electric hand mixer was used for mixing only when mixer speeds are specified in the recipe directions. When a mixer speed is not given, a spoon or fork was used.

Cooking Terms Glossary

Beat: Mix ingredients vigorously with spoon, fork, wire whisk, hand beater or electric mixer until smooth and uniform.

Boil: Heat liquid until bubbles rise continuously and break on the surface and steam is given off. For rolling boil, the bubbles form rapidly.

Chop: Cut into coarse or fine irregular pieces with a knife, food chopper, blender or food processor.

Cube: Cut into squares ½ inch or larger.

Dice: Cut into squares smaller than ½ inch.

Grate: Cut into tiny particles using small rough holes of grater (citrus peel or chocolate).

Grease: Rub the inside surface of a pan with shortening, using pastry brush, piece of waxed paper or paper towel, to prevent food from sticking during baking (as for some casseroles).

Julienne: Cut into thin, matchlike strips, using knife or food processor (vegetables, fruits, meats).

Mix: Combine ingredients in any way that distributes them evenly.

Sauté: Cook foods in hot oil or margarine over medium-high heat with frequent tossing and turning motion.

Shred: Cut into long thin pieces by rubbing food across the holes of a shredder, as for cheese, or by using a knife to slice very thinly, as for cabbage.

Simmer: Cook in liquid just below the boiling point on top of the stove; usually after reducing heat from a boil. Bubbles will rise slowly and break just below the surface.

Stir: Mix ingredients until uniform consistency. Stir once in a while for stirring occasionally, often for stirring frequently and continuously for stirring constantly.

Toss: Tumble ingredients (such as green salad) lightly with a lifting motion, usually to coat evenly or mix with another food.

metric conversion guide

Volume

U.S. Units	Canadian Metric	Australian Metric
¼ teaspoon	1 mL	1 ml
½ teaspoon	2 mL	2 ml
1 teaspoon	5 mL	5 ml
1 tablespoon	15 mL	20 ml
¼ cup	50 mL	60 ml
⅓ cup	75 mL	80 ml
½ cup	125 mL	125 ml
⅔ cup	150 mL	170 ml
¾ cup	175 mL	190 ml
1 cup	250 mL	250 ml
1 quart	1 liter	1 liter
1½ quarts	1.5 liters	1.5 liters
2 quarts	2 liters	2 liters
2½ quarts	2.5 liters	2.5 liters
3 quarts	3 liters	3 liters
4 quarts	4 liters	4 liters

Weight

U.S. Units	Canadian Metric	Australian Metric
¼ teaspoon	1 mL	1 ml
1 ounce	30 grams	30 grams
2 ounces	55 grams	60 grams
3 ounces	85 grams	90 grams
4 ounces (¼ pound)	115 grams	125 grams
8 ounces (½ pound)	225 grams	225 grams
16 ounces (1 pound)	455 grams	500 grams
1 pound	455 grams	½ kilogram

Note: The recipes in this cookbook have not been developed or tested using metric measures. When converting recipes to metric, some variations in quality may be noted.

Measurements

Inches	Centimeters
1	2.5
2	5.0
3	7.5
4	10.0
5	12.5
6	15.0
7	17.5
8	20.5
9	23.0
10	25.5
11	28.0
12	30.5
13	33.0

Temperatures

Fahrenheit	Celsius
32°	0°
212°	100°
250°	120°
275°	140°
300°	150°
325°	160°
350°	180°
375°	190°
400°	200°
425°	220°
450°	230°
475°	240°
500°	260°

index

Note: *Italicized* page references indicate photographs.

Hungry for more?

See what else Pillsbury has to offer.

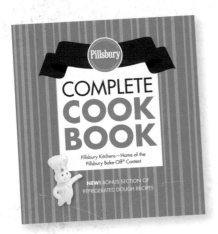